D1403056

DECORATIVE
PAINTING
COLOR
MATCH
SOURCEBOOK

TCS®

DECORATIVE PAINTING COLOR MATCH SOURCEBOOK

Updated Edition

The complete guide to finding color matches for every top brand of paint

BOBBIE PEARCY

Tru-Color Systems
Danville, Indiana

Decorative Painting Color Match Sourcebook©

Other Tru-Color Products: www.gotcs.com

Printed in China by Everbest Printing Co. through
      Four Colour Imports, Ltd.,
      Louisville, KY
      www.fourcolour.com

Distributed to the trade and art markets in North America by
      North Light Books, in imprint of
      F & W Publications, Inc.
      1507 Dana Avenue
      Cincinnati, Ohio 45207
      1-800-289-0963

TCS is the registered trademark ® of
Tru-Color Systems, Inc.

Tru-Color Systems, Inc.
64 E. Marion St. • P.O. Box 486
Danville, IN 46122-0486
Phone: (317) 745-7535 Fax: (317) 745-1886
E-mail: comments@gotcs.com

Table of Contents

Introduction

No matter which brand of paints you use, there will always be references to colors which you do not have available to you. Magazines and pattern books use hundreds of color names which often must be matched to complete the project as the author intended.

The *TCS Decorative Painting Color Match Sourcebook* is designed to assist you in selecting matching colors from various brands. Where a perfect match is not available, a mix is provided. Each suggested mix includes the mixing ratio and a printed swatch of the target color.

OIL AND ACRYLIC CONVERSIONS!

Oil painters may now choose acrylic projects even though they do not recognize the color names. Look up any acrylic name and find one or more oil matches. 220 familiar oil color names have matches in acrylic brands.

And acrylic painters are free to use any of the beautiful oil patterns available.

OUR THANKS!

We are indebted to the artists who have assisted us with color mixes and paint swatches. We offer our sincere "thanks" to Ginger Edwards, Jenny Fennewald, Maureen McNaughton, Cheri Rol, and Vi Thurmond for their willingness to share their artistic skills and talents.

Several leading magazine publishers choose to include the TCS System with their designs. *The Decorative Painter*, *Decorative Artist's Workbook* and *Paintworks* magazines provide the TCS System in each issue as a service to their readers.

In addition, the many authors who publish with Blue Ridge Publications, Sharon & Gayle and several independent designers include the TCS identifiers so their customers can be assured of finding the correct color for their projects, no matter the color name, oil or acrylic. We thank them all for their continuing support.

Continued Success!

Bobbie Pearcy

As a decorative painting teacher, Bobbie Pearcy had a dilemma. How to help her students understand the differences among the various color names. It can be very confusing because the paint brands sometimes have different names for the same color and/or the same name for different colors.

As a result, she created the TCS Color Matching System, which is widely accepted as the industry standard solution for color conversions. It is also available in a computer software program.

In addition, she authored the *Tru-Color Teaching Guide and Session Planner* for those who wish to further develop their artistic skills by organizing a program to teach others.

FEATURING TWENTY-ONE BRANDS

Twenty-One (21) brands of oil, acrylic, and fabric paints are featured in the TCS Color Match System. The sheer volume of information limits the index in this sourcebook to nine (9) brands, However, additional brands in color name order, with TCS#'s, are available from the internet.

If your favorite brand is not included in this index, you may print TCS information for additional brands from our web page: www.gotcs.com

How to Use This Book

The *TCS Decorative Painting Color Match Sourcebook* is designed for quick access to color matches in an easy-to-use format. Each box in this book represents one specific color. It is composed of either matching colors in different brands of paint, or creating mixes to match the target color for that TCS number. This means you can use your favorite brand of paint to complete any project you choose, regardless of the brands designated in the pattern.

A Choose a color name from the table of contents (page 5), the alphabetic index (pages 91-98) or use the color bars along the sides of pages.

The color bars are grouped by color families, starting with Yellow. They represent the first color shown on the page and can in turn help you find the approximate location of a color when you are not sure of the color name, but you know, for instance, that it is a yellow color. From there, look at the color names listed in the bar; they represent the first and last color on that page.

B Turn to the listed page and TCS number or to a page where the color bar represents the color family you are looking for.

C There you will find six colors and/or mixes including your target color if you've gone the route of the alphabetic list. Suggested shades and highlights are located under the color name.

A sample color box:

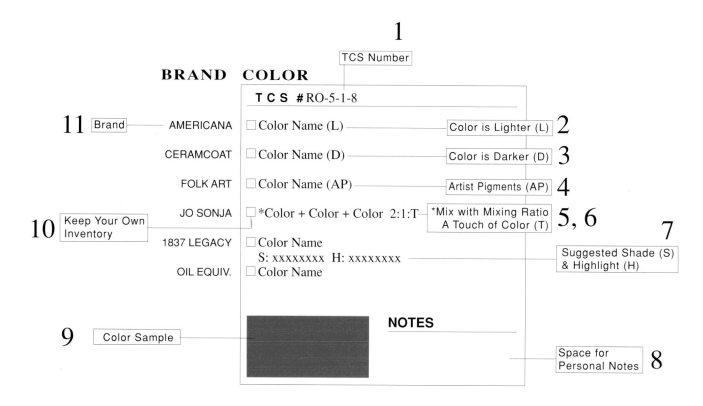

Here's how to read the sample color box:

1 **TCS Number.** Always located in the upper left corner. It identifies the unique color qualities which these six colors/mixes have in common.

The TCS numbering system is designed to give you more options in your color choices. You can find a very close color to your target color by working with the last digit of the TCS number–the value of the color. For instance, all of the colors numbered BL-6-1-1 through BL-6-1-9 are the same in hue and clarity. They differ only in value. So, if you do not have Ocean Reef Blue (TCS number BL-6-1-5) or any of its matches, look at the box before or after to find the closest color. In this case, any color or mix in TCS number BL-6-1-4 or BL-6-1-6 would work as a substitute. The hue and clarity are the same, and only the value of the color is a slight shade lighter or darker

2 **An (L) After the Name** indicates the color is a shade lighter than the represented color. In most cases this color will work as well as the color called for in the pattern. To darken the color to match the representative color, add a touch of a darker color in the same color family, or black, to the designated color.

3 **A Color with a (D)** after it means that color is a shade darker than the represented color. Again, this color will suffice in most cases. To lighten the color to match the representative color, add a touch of a lighter color in the same color family to the designated color–or you may add a touch of white.

4 **(AP)** at the end of a Folk Art color indicates it is one of their Artist Pigments colors. These paints, made of artist-grade pigments, are highly concentrated to give better coverage.

5 **Color Mixes are Prefaced With an Asterisk (*).** Many of the colors from different brands do not perfectly match colors from other brands. When this occurs, we want you to know how to accurately match a pattern's given color, so we give you the recipe for a mix to duplicate that color. This mix is written with colors from the brand you have chosen for your color match. For instance, the color called for in the pattern: Delta Ceramcoat - Tangerine.

The sourcebook lists a mix for Jo Sonja of *Vermillion + Yellow Light 4:1. This means that by mixing four (4) parts of Jo Sonja's Vermillion with one (1) part of her Yellow Light you will have a color which matches Ceramcoat's Tangerine

All mixes are listed with a ratio mixing formula: the first number in the formula referring to the first color in the mix, the second number corresponding with the second color, etc.

6 **A Color Within a Mix** designated with a **(T)** after it means that adding a "touch" (lightly tip the corner of the brush in the "touch" color and add it to the color/mix) will give you a very accurate match.

*Examples: *Orange + Red (T) means add just a touch of Red to the Orange.*

*White + Red + Orange 1:1:T means mix equal parts White and Red then add a "touch" of Orange

7 **Shades and Highlights.** Some of the brands have a suggested shade and highlight for each of their standard colors. For quick reference, they are printed under the color name. Please note this is only one set of many shades and highlights which could be used for each color.

8 **Personal Notes.** We have provided space for your personal notes in each match block. If you have a mix you prefer for this color, write it here.

9 **Color Sample.** Representative color which equals all paints and mixes in this TCS box.

10 **Record Your Inventory.** Beside each color name is a small box which you can mark to indicate you have the color(s) in your inventory.

Understanding the TCS Color Classification System

Remember, you can match all the colors of the leading brands without reference to the TCS number. However, by understanding this number, you can add more versatility to your painting.

The TCS identifier divides the complete color spectrum into fifteen color families. All colors and mixes are identified by a two-character alphabetic abbreviation and a unique three-digit number. Each number is based on a scale of nine segments. It is helpful to familiarize yourself with the abbreviations and color class they represent.

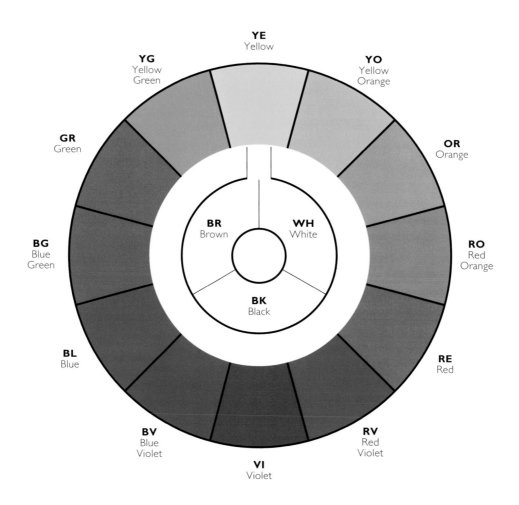

TCS Color Family Identifiers

YE = Yellow	**BL** = Blue
YO = Yellow Orange	**BG** = Blue Green
OR = Orange	**GR** = Green
RO = Red Orange	**YG** = Yellow Green
RE = Red	**BR** = Brown
RV = Red Violet	**BK** = Black
VI = Violet	**WH** = White
BV = Blue Violet	

Learn to Use the TCS Number:
Color Family-Hue-Clarity-Value

The individual TCS number assigned to a color identifies the following:

TCS # BL-5-7-4
Color Family   Hue   Clarity   Value

COLOR FAMILY

Two alpha characters which identify the color family of the color—YE (Yellow), YO (Yellow Orange), OR (Orange), etc.

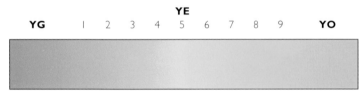

COLOR HUE

This indicates the position of a color in its color family. Each color family is segmented into nine parts. Reading clockwise from 1 (which is closer to the color on the color wheel before it) to 9 (closer to the family listed after it) with 5 being closest to the pure color of that family. Example: A yellow #8 (YE-8) would be much closer to yellow orange or a yellow with an orange cast, and a yellow #3 (YE-3) would be a yellow with a touch of green (closer to yellow green).

COLOR CLARITY

Color clarity or intensity is identified with 1 being a very bright, clear color to 9 being a very grayed color. Adding a small amount of the complement color to a bright color will gray or mud the color. The exact opposite color on the color wheel is the complementary color: i.e., red is the complement of green. When two colors are in the same color fam-

ily, with the same hue but the clarity (second number) of one is much higher than the other, note the variance in clarity of the colors:

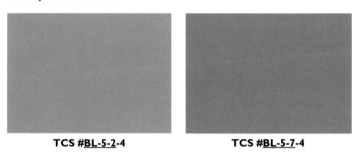

TCS #BL-5-2-4   **TCS #BL-5-7-4**

COLOR VALUE

This again segmented into nine different sections to describe the relative position of the color on a gray scale where 1 is a light/pastel color and 9 is very dark. Example: White is a 1 and Black is a 9.

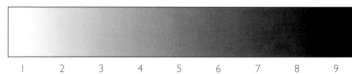

So, a color identified as BL-5-7-4 would indicate the color is in the blue family (BL), is a pure hue with no violet or green tones (5); is quite grayed (7); and is slightly lighter than a medium value (4). (See page 51 for all six brands of this color.)

TCS #BL-5-7-4

How to Mix Paint

It is easy to mix paint. Just like measuring and mixing the ingredients called for in a favorite recipe, you will get accurate mixes by using the measurements of ingredients (paint) called for in a color mix. However, you do not need your measuring cups and spoons to make the measurements exact. If you can squeeze out puddles of paint of like size, you can use these to create the ratios of paint in any mix. For example, if the color is:

Bright Red + Yellow 3:1

Squeeze out three parts (puddles) of bright red and one part (puddle) of yellow next to each other on your palette and mix together with your palette knife or brush. The size of the puddles depends on how much of a color you need to mix.

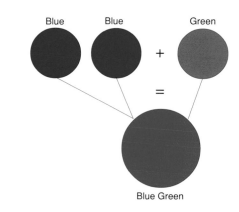

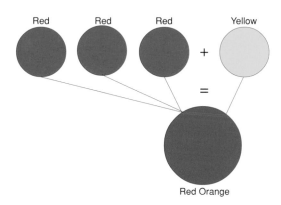

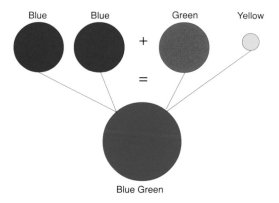

Remember the first number in the ratio refers to the first color in the mix, the second refers to the second, and so on.

When a mix calls for a touch (T) of a color, this touch of paint can be eliminated without harming the end result of the project. For example:

Blue + Green + Yellow 2:1:T

If you mix two puddles of blue with one puddle of green, the resulting color will be "almost" perfect. The purist may add just a touch of yellow to get the *exact* color the project calls for.

In creating these mixes, we start with the lighter color and add the darker or more intense color(s) a little at a time. That is because darker values will color the mix faster and there is less opportunity to pass the desired shade required. By starting with several very small puddles of the paint we need for a specific color, we add a small amount of the darker shade to the lighter color, comparing it with the original color of the TCS number until we have a match. We paint a swatch, make note of the mixing recipe we used, then, if it is still a match when dry, we record the information. Although there are usually many mixes to match a color, we try to choose the simplest ones possible. One theory we use when mixing colors is: Any two colors can be used to mix a color between them.

Since we have already created and tested the color match recipes in this book, you can simply mix the paints in the amounts stated and get the right results.

Please note: You can mix a small amount of paint with your brush. However you must take care to keep the paint out of the ferrule (the metal part that holds the brushes in place). If paint dries underneath the ferrule, your brush will be ruined. For larger quantities of paint it is safer to use a palette knife.

Brands & Contact Information

BRANDS LISTED IN THE SOURCEBOOK INDEX

ACRYLIC

Americana™
DecoArt, Inc.
P.O. Box 386, Stanford, KY 40484
Phone: (800) 367-3047 Fax: (606) 365-9739

Ceramcoat®
Delta Technical Coatings, Inc.
2550 Pellissier Place, Whittier, CA 90601-1505
Phone: (800) 423-4135 Fax: (310) 695-5157

Folk Art®
Plaid Enterprises, Inc.
1649 International Court
P.O. Box 7600, Norcross, GA 30091
Phone: (770) 923-8200 Fax: (770) 381-3404

Jo Sonja®
Chroma, Inc.
205 Bucky Drive, Lititz, PA 17543
Phone: (800) 257-8278 Fax: (717) 626-9292

1837 Legacy™
TCS # printed on every label
Maple Ridge Paint Co.
P.O. Box 14, Ridgetown, Ontario N0P 2C0
Canada
Phone: (888) 214-0062 Fax: (888) 214-0062
e-mail: info@1837legacy.com

OIL

Archival® *Oils*   (ACR)
Chroma, Inc.
205 Bucky Drive, Lititz, PA 17543
Phone: (800) 257-8278 Fax: (717) 626-9292

Prima® *Oils*   (PRI)
Martin/F. Weber Co.
2727 Southhampton Road,
Philadelphia, PA 19154-1293
Phone: (215) 677-5600 Fax:(215) 677-3336

Rembrandt® *Oils*   (REM)
Canson-Talens, Inc.
21 Industrial Drive, P.O. Box 220,
South Hadley, MA 01075
Phone: (800) 628-9283 Fax: (413) 533-6554

Winsor & Newton® *Oils*   (WN)
ColArt Americas, Inc.
11 Constitution Avenue, P.O. Box 1396
Piscataway, NJ 08855-1396
Phone: (800) 445-4278 Fax: (732) 562-0941

TO FIND INDEXES OF THESE BRANDS
www.gotcs.com

Genesis® *Artist Colors International*
Heat-Set Artist Oils
The Fine Arts Div. American Art Clay Co., Inc.
4717 W. 16th Street, Indianapolis, IN 46222
Phone: (800) 374-1600 Fax: (317) 248-9300

Liquitex® *Oils*** *and Acrylics*
Binney & Smith
1100 Church Lane, P.O. Box 431
Easton, PA 18044
Phone: (800) 272-9652 Fax (610) 559-9007

Holbein Duo Aqua Oils & Acryla Gouache
H. K. Holbein
20 Commerce St., P.O. Box 555
Williston, VT 05495
Phone: (800) 682-6686 Fax: (802) 658-5889

Aleene's® *Acrylic & Tulip*® *Fabric Paints*
Duncan Enterprises
5673 E. Shields Avenue, Fresno, CA 93727
Phone: (800) 438-6226 Fax: (209) 291-9444

Accent® *Acrylics & Max*® *Oils*
Sanford, Art and Education Division.
2711 Washington, Bellwood, IL 60104
Phone (800) 323-0749

Apple Barrel® *Acrylics*
See Plaid Enterprises

Delta® *Fabric Paints*
See Delta Technical Coatings

Prima® *Acrylics & Permalba*® *Oils*
See Martin/F. Weber Co.

**Liquitex Oils are discontinued. Because of the many painting projects referencing this popular oil medium, we have established TCS Color identifiers and placed them on our internet page. The TCS System allows conversions to other oil or acrylic brands.

NEW COLORS

As new colors are introduced and brands added, they will appear first on our web page. Check there to obtain updates.

www.gotcs.com

Using the Color Match Project Planner

O n the project planner:
- List the colors named in the pattern, along with brand.
- Locate these colors in the alphabetic index and note the page and TCS number of each color.
- Turn to the listed page and TCS number.

- You have a choice of six matching colors and/or mixes including your original color. Check your personal inventory boxes to determine if you have the color needed. Any color or mix in that TCS number box can be substituted for the original color.

For example:

COLOR MATCH PROJECT PLANNER

PROJECT NAME ___Kit Kat (a wall hung broom holder)___ SUBJECT ___Animals___

PROJECT SOURCE (OR DESIGNING ARTIST) ___a pattern packet by Jane Doe___

BRAND	COLOR REQUESTED	PAGE #	TCS #	COLOR MATCH
Folk Art	Settler's Blue	42	BL-5-7-4	Ceramcoat Cape Cod
Folk Art	Denim Blue	43	BL-5-7-8	Ceramcoat Nightfall
Folk Art	Poppy Red	22	RE-3-2-6	Jo Sonja Rose Pk + Vermillion 3:1
Ceramcoat	Golden Brown	61	BR-1-2-4	In Inventory

COLOR MATCH PROJECT PLANNER

PROJECT NAME _____ SUBJECT _____

PROJECT SOURCE (OR DESIGNING ARTIST) _____

BRAND	COLOR REQUESTED	PAGE #	TCS #	COLOR MATCH

COLOR MATCH PROJECT PLANNER

PROJECT NAME _____ SUBJECT _____

PROJECT SOURCE (OR DESIGNING ARTIST) _____

BRAND	COLOR REQUESTED	PAGE #	TCS #	COLOR MATCH

COLOR MATCH PROJECT PLANNER

PROJECT NAME _____ SUBJECT _____

PROJECT SOURCE (OR DESIGNING ARTIST) _____

BRAND	COLOR REQUESTED	PAGE #	TCS #	COLOR MATCH

BRAND	COLOR	COLOR

T C S # YE-2-4-2

AMERICANA	☐ *Lemon Yellow + Olive Green 1:1
CERAMCOAT	☐ *Pineapple Yellow + Lime Green (T)
FOLK ART	☐ *Lemon Custard + Clover (T)
JO SONJA	☐ *Cadmium Yellow Light + Moss Green 8:1
1837 LEGACY	☐ Barley S: Light Yellow Green H: Maize
OIL EQUIV.	☐ WN Lemon Yellow Hue

NOTES

T C S # YE-2-4-5

☐ Olde Gold S: Antique Green H: Golden Straw
☐ Mustard S: Cloudberry H: Pineapple
☐ *Yellow Ochre + Porcelain White 8:1
☐ *Turner's Yellow + Smoked Pearl 1:1
☐ *Caribou + Moss 6:1
☐ *WN Yellow Ochre + Olive Green + Cadmium Yellow + White 4:2:1:2

NOTES

T C S # YE-4-1-1

AMERICANA	☐ *Taffy Cream + White 2:1
CERAMCOAT	☐ *Custard + White 2:1
FOLK ART	☐ Buttercream S: Yellow Ochre H: Wicker White
JO SONJA	☐ *Warm White + Yellow Light 2:1
1837 LEGACY	☐ Maize S: Daffodil H: White
OIL EQUIV.	☐ *WN White + Cadmium Yellow Pale 10:1

NOTES

T C S # YE-4-1-2

☐ Pineapple S: Olde Gold H: Light Buttermilk
☐ Pale Yellow S: Butter Yellow H: White
☐ *Lemon Custard + Buttercream (T)
☐ *Warm White + Yellow Light (T)
☐ Canola S: Hansa Yellow   H: White
☐ *WN White + Cadmium Yellow Pale 3:1

NOTES

T C S # YE-4-1-3

AMERICANA	☐ *White + Lemon Yellow 1:1
CERAMCOAT	☐ Sunbright Yellow S: Butter Yellow H: White
FOLK ART	☐ *Lemon Custard + White 3:1
JO SONJA	☐ *Cadmium Yellow Light + Warm White 1:1
1837 LEGACY	☐ Banana Cream S: Golden Rod H: Maize
OIL EQUIV.	☐ *WN White + CadmiumYellow Pale 20:3

NOTES

T C S # YE-4-1-4

☐ Lemon Yellow S: Olde Gold H: Light Buttermilk
☐ Luscious Lemon S: Yellow H: Pale Yellow
☐ Lemon Custard S: Yellow Ochre H: White
☐ Cadmium Yellow Light
☐ Sunflower S: Sungold H: Maize
☐ ARC Cadmium Yellow Light, REM Cadmium Yellow Light, WN Cadmium Lemon

NOTES

BRAND	COLOR	COLOR

T C S # YE-4-1-5

AMERICANA	☐ *Cadmium Yellow + Lemon Yellow 1:1
CERAMCOAT	☐ Opaque Yellow S: Antique Gold H: Pale Yellow
FOLK ART	☐ Medium Yellow (AP) S: Yellow Ochre H: Lemonade
JO SONJA	☐ Cadmium Yellow Mid. (D)
1837 LEGACY	☐ *Dandelion + Sunflower 2:1
OIL EQUIV.	☐ ARC Superchrome Yellow Light, WN Cadmium Yellow Pale

NOTES

T C S # YE-5-1-5

☐ Yellow Light S: Raw Sienna H: Pineapple
☐ Bright Yellow S: Empire Gold H: Pale Yellow
☐ Yellow Light (AP) (D) S: Yellow Ochre H: White
☐ Yellow Light
☐ Hansa Yellow S: Golden Rod H: Canola
☐ ARC Yellow Light, WN Winsor Lemon

NOTES

T C S # YE-5-1-6

AMERICANA	☐ Cadmium Yellow S: Terra Cotta H: Pineapple
CERAMCOAT	☐ *Bright Yellow + Yellow 1:1
FOLK ART	☐ Yellow Light (AP) S: Yellow Ochre H: White
JO SONJA	☐ Cadmium Yellow Mid
1837 LEGACY	☐ *Hansa Yellow + Dandelion 1:1
OIL EQUIV.	☐ ARC Cadmium Yellow Mid., WN Chrome Yellow Hue

NOTES

T C S # YE-5-1-7

☐ Primary Yellow S: Antique Gold H: Pineapple
☐ Yellow S: Pigskin H: Custard
☐ School Bus Yellow S: Raw Sienna H: Warm White
☐ Cadmium Yellow Medium (L)
☐ Dandelion S: Yellow Oxide H: Canola
☐ ARC Superchrome Yellow Mid., PRI Cadmium Yellow Light Hue, REM Cadmium Yellow Medium

NOTES

T C S # YE-5-2-3

AMERICANA	☐ *Pineapple + Lemon Yellow (T)
CERAMCOAT	☐ Pineapple Yellow S: Antique Gold H: White
FOLK ART	☐ *Lemon Custard + White 1:1
JO SONJA	☐ *Yellow Light + Warm White 1:1
1837 LEGACY	☐ Daffodil S: Caribou H: Maize
OIL EQUIV.	☐ WN Transparent Yellow

NOTES

T C S # YE-5-4-5

☐ *True Ochre + White 1:1
☐ Butter Yellow S: Pigskin H: Ivory
☐ Turner's Yellow (AP) S: Yellow Ochre H: Sunflower
☐ *Turner's Yellow + White 3:1
☐ Sungold S: Yellow Oxide H: Lemon Meringue
☐ *WN Cadmium Yellow + White + Yellow Ochre 2:1:1

NOTES

BRAND	COLOR	COLOR

T C S # YE-5-5-2

AMERICANA	☐ *White + Golden Straw 2:1
CERAMCOAT	☐ *White + Straw 2:1
FOLK ART	☐ Sunflower S: Yellow Ochre H: Buttercream
JO SONJA	☐ *White + Turner's Yellow 4:1
1837 LEGACY	☐ *White + Caribou 2:1
OIL EQUIV.	☐ *WN Naples Yellow + White 2:1

NOTES

T C S # YE-5-5-5

☐ Golden Straw
  S: Honey Brown H: Moon Yellow
☐ Straw
  S: Golden Brown H: Ivory
☐ Buttercup
  S: Yellow Ochre H: White
☐ *Opal + Turner's Yellow 5:1

☐ Caribou
  S: Yellow Oxide H: Maize
☐ *WN White + Cadmium Yellow Pale + Alizarin
  Crimson + Ultramarine Blue 10:3:1:1

NOTES

T C S # YE-6-2-1

AMERICANA	☐ *White + Taffy Cream 1:1
CERAMCOAT	☐ Cornsilk Yellow S: Pale Yellow H: White
FOLK ART	☐ *Lemonade + White 1:1
JO SONJA	☐ *White + Cadmium Yellow Light 5:1
1837 LEGACY	☐ *Lemon Meringue + White 1:1
OIL EQUIV.	☐ *WN White + Cadmium Lemon 4:1

NOTES

T C S # YE-6-2-2

☐ Taffy Cream
  S: Golden Straw H: White
☐ Custard
  S: Butter Yellow H: White
☐ Lemonade
  S: Yellow Ochre H: White
☐ *White + Yellow Light 3:1

☐ Lemon Meringue
  S: Margarine H: White
☐ REM Naples Yellow Light,
  WN Naples Yellow Light

NOTES

T C S # YE-6-2-4

AMERICANA	☐ *Cadmium Yellow + White 1:1
CERAMCOAT	☐ Crocus Yellow S: Antique Gold H: Light Ivory
FOLK ART	☐ *White + School Bus Yellow 3:1
JO SONJA	☐ *White + Turner's Yellow 3:1
1837 LEGACY	☐ *Margarine + Sungold 1:1
OIL EQUIV.	☐ WN Winsor Yellow

NOTES

T C S # YE-6-2-6

☐ Marigold
  S: Raw Sienna H: Golden Straw
☐ Empire Gold
  S: Mocha Brown H: Crocus Yellow
☐ *Medium Yellow + Pure Orange (T)

☐ Turner's Yellow

☐ Golden Rod
  S: Yellow Oxide H: Daffodil
☐ WN Aureolin

NOTES

T C S # YE-6-4-5

AMERICANA ☐ Antique Gold
S: Raw Sienna H: Golden Straw
CERAMCOAT ☐ Antique Gold
S: Raw Sienna H: Ivory
FOLK ART ☐ Yellow Ochre (AP)
S: English Mustard H: Lemonade
JO SONJA ☐ Yellow Oxide (D)

1837 LEGACY ☐ Yellow Oxide (D)
S: Mocha H: Margarine
OIL EQUIV. ☐ ARC Yellow Ochre,
REM Yellow Ochre Light
WN Mars Yellow

NOTES

T C S # YE-6-4-7

☐ True Ochre
S: Burnt Umber H: Golden Straw
☐ Antique Gold (L)
S: Raw Sienna H: Ivory
☐ Yellow Ochre (AP) (L)
S: English Mustard H: Lemonade
☐ Yellow Oxide

☐ Yellow Oxide
S: Mocha H: Margarine
☐ WN Yellow Ochre Pale

NOTES

T C S # YE-6-4-8

AMERICANA ☐ *True Ochre + Raw Sienna (T)

CERAMCOAT ☐ Pigskin
S: Autumn Brown H: Butter Yellow
FOLK ART ☐ *Yellow Ochre + English Mustard 1:1

JO SONJA ☐ *Yellow Oxide + Raw Sienna (T)

1837 LEGACY ☐ Tigereye
S: Mocha H: Margarine
OIL EQUIV. ☐ WN Yellow Ochre

NOTES

T C S # YE-7-7-2

☐ *Taffy Cream + Moon Yellow 3:1

☐ Mello Yellow
S: Straw H: Light Ivory
☐ *French Vanilla + Lemon Custard 8:1

☐ *Warm White + Yellow Oxide 8:1

☐ *Lemon Meringue + Margarine 2:1

☐ PRI Naples Yellow Hue

NOTES

T C S # YE-7-7-3

AMERICANA ☐ Moon Yellow
S: Honey Brown H: Taffy
CERAMCOAT ☐ Old Parchment
S: Spice Tan H: Light Ivory
FOLK ART ☐ Moon Yellow (Disc.) or
*Sunflower + Buttercup 3:1
JO SONJA ☐ Naples Yellow Hue or
Jo Sonja Bkg Primrose
1837 LEGACY ☐ Margarine
S: Yellow Oxide H: Lemon Meringue
OIL EQUIV. ☐ *WN White + Cadmium Yellow Pale +
Bright Red 10:3:1

NOTES

T C S # YE-7-7-4

☐ Moon Yellow (L)
S: Honey Brown H: Taffy
☐ Maple Sugar Tan
S: Burnt Sienna H: Ivory
☐ Buttercrunch
S: English Mustard H: White
☐ *Yellow Oxide + Warm White 1:1

☐ Chamois
S: Doeskin H: Devon Cream
☐ *WN Naples Yellow + White + AlizarinCrimson
+Ultramarine Blue 10:2:1:1

NOTES

BRAND   COLOR   COLOR

T C S # YE-7-7-6

AMERICANA	☐ Yellow Ochre S: Honey Brown H: Moon Yellow
CERAMCOAT	☐ *Old Parchment + Spice Tan 5:1
FOLK ART	☐ *Sunflower + Teddy Bear Tan 6:1
JO SONJA	☐ *Warm White + Yellow Oxide + Fawn 10:1:T
1837 LEGACY	☐ *Warm Beige + Barley 5:1
OIL EQUIV.	☐ *WN White + Yellow Ochre 2:1

NOTES

T C S # YO-5-1-4

☐ Tangerine S: Terra Cotta H: Lemon Yellow	
☐ *Yellow + Bittersweet 3:1	
☐ *Medium Yellow + Pure Orange 3:1	
☐ Indian Yellow	
☐ *Dandelion + Mango 3:1	
☐ ARC Arylomide Yellow Deep, REM Stil De Grain Jaune, WN Indian Yellow	

NOTES

T C S # YO-5-2-4

AMERICANA	☐ *Primary Yellow + Tangerine 2:1
CERAMCOAT	☐ *Yellow + Pumpkin 4:1
FOLK ART	☐ *School Bus Yellow + Tangerine 2:1
JO SONJA	☐ Yellow Deep
1837 LEGACY	☐ *Hansa Yellow + Duck Bill 4:1
OIL EQUIV.	☐ WN Cadmium Yellow

NOTES

T C S # YO-6-1-1

☐ *Sand + Medium Flesh (T)	
☐ Western Sunset Yellow S: Mocha Brown H: Putty	
☐ *Wicker White + Peach Cobbler 3:1	
☐ *Warm White + Yellow Oxide + Vermillion 10:1:T	
☐ Wheat S: Raw Sienna H: Ecru	
☐ ARC Jaune Brillant, *WN White + Jaune Brillant 2:1	

NOTES

T C S # YO-6-1-3

AMERICANA	☐ *Tangerine + Moon Yellow 2:1
CERAMCOAT	☐ Calypso Orange S: Dark Goldenrod H: Western Sunset Yellow
FOLK ART	☐ *Tangerine + White 4:1
JO SONJA	☐ *Cad Yellow Light + Vermillion 8:1
1837 LEGACY	☐ *White + Duck Bill 3:1
OIL EQUIV.	☐ *WN Cadmium Yellow Deep + White 3:1

NOTES

T C S # YO-6-1-5

☐ *Tangerine + Pumpkin (T)	
☐ *Yellow + Pumpkin 1:1	
☐ Tangerine S: Burnt Sienna H: Sunny Yellow	
☐ *Cadmium Yellow Mid + Vermillion 8:1	
☐ *Dandelion + Duck Bill 1:1	
☐ PRI Cadmium Yellow Medium Hue, WN Cadmium Yellow Deep	

NOTES

BRAND	COLOR	COLOR

T C S # OR-3-1-4

AMERICANA	☐ *Peaches 'n Cream + Pumpkin 3:1
CERAMCOAT	☐ *Pink Angel + Pumpkin 3:1
FOLK ART	☐ *Skintone + Tangerine 1:1
JO SONJA	☐ Jaune Brillant
1837 LEGACY	☐ *Natural Blush + Duck Bill 3:1
OIL EQUIV.	☐ WN Jaune Brillant

NOTES

T C S # OR-4-1-5

☐ *Tangerine + Cadmium Orange (T)

☐ Bittersweet Orange
S: Terra Cotta H: Yellow
☐ Glazed Carrots
S: Light Red Oxide H: White
☐ *Cadmium Yellow Mid. + Cadmium Scarlet 2:1

☐ Mango
S: Mocha H: Wheat
☐ ARC Indian Yellow

NOTES

T C S # OR-4-2-1

AMERICANA	☐ *Sand + Toffee 5:1
CERAMCOAT	☐ Queen Anne's Lace S: Rosetta H: White
FOLK ART	☐ *Georgia Peach + Taffy 1:1
JO SONJA	☐ *Warm White + Yellow Oxide + Vermillion 12:1:T
1837 LEGACY	☐ *Creamette + Maiden's Blush (T)
OIL EQUIV.	☐ *WN White + Jaune Brillant 4:1

NOTES

T C S # OR-4-7-3

☐ *Medium Flesh + Burnt Orange 12:1

☐ *Dark Goldenrod + Old Parchment 4:1

☐ *Raw Sienna + French Vanilla 4:1

☐ *Warm White + Yellow Oxide +
Norwegian Orange 6:1:1
☐ Cool Peach
S: Burnt Sienna H: Natural Blush
☐ *WN Jaune Brillant + Raw Sienna 5:1

NOTES

T C S # OR-4-7-4

AMERICANA	☐ *Tangerine + Terra Cotta 2:1
CERAMCOAT	☐ Dark Goldenrod S: Terra Cotta H: Calypso Orange
FOLK ART	☐ *Raw Sienna + Yellow Ochre 3:1
JO SONJA	☐ *Turner's Yellow + Gold Oxide 8:1
1837 LEGACY	☐ *Mocha + Maize 1:1
OIL EQUIV.	☐ *WN Cadmium Yellow Deep + Burnt Umber 4:1

NOTES

T C S # OR-4-7-6

☐ *Terra Cotta + Burnt Orange 3:1

☐ Terra Cotta
S: Brown Iron Oxide H: Island Coral
☐ *Glazed Carrots + English Mustard 2:1

☐ Gold Oxide (D)

☐ Pumpkin Pie
S: Burnt Sienna H: Mango
☐ *WN Yellow Ochre + REM Geranium Lake +
WN Burnt Sienna 3:2:1

NOTES

BRAND   **COLOR**   **COLOR**

T C S # OR-4-7-8

AMERICANA	☐ *Burnt Orange + Burnt Sienna (T)
CERAMCOAT	☐ *Mocha Brown + Raw Sienna 1:1
FOLK ART	☐ *Autumn Leaves + Buckskin Brown 1:1
JO SONJA	☐ Gold Oxide
1837 LEGACY	☐ *Mocha + Raw Sienna 1:1
OIL EQUIV.	☐ ARC Gold Ochre

NOTES

T C S # OR-4-7-9

☐ *Burnt Orange + Burnt Sienna 5:1

☐ Cinnamon
S: Sonoma H: Santa Fe Rose
☐ *Teddy Bear Brown + Autumn Leaves 1:1

☐ *Gold Oxide + Red Earth 1:1

☐ *Brick + Burgundy 2:1

☐ WN Venetian Red

NOTES

T C S # OR-5-1-4

AMERICANA	☐ *Pumpkin + White 1:1
CERAMCOAT	☐ *Pumpkin + White 1:1
FOLK ART	☐ Orange Light S: Medium Orange H: Georgia Peach
JO SONJA	☐ *White + Cadmium Orange 3:1
1837 LEGACY	☐ *Fresh Tangerine + White 1:1
OIL EQUIV.	☐ *WN Cadmium Orange + White 2:1

NOTES

T C S # OR-5-1-5

☐ Pumpkin
S: Burnt Sienna H: Cadmium Yellow
☐ Pumpkin
S: Georgia Clay H: Yellow
☐ Medium Orange
S: Red Light H: Bright Peach
☐ *Vermillion + Yellow Light 3:1

☐ Duck Bill
S: Burnt Clay H: Sunflower
☐ ARC Cadmium Orange,
WN Cadmium Orange

NOTES

T C S # OR-5-2-1

AMERICANA	☐ *Buttermilk + Flesh 3:1
CERAMCOAT	☐ Putty S: Dresden Flesh H: White
FOLK ART	☐ *Taffy + Georgia Peach 1:1
JO SONJA	☐ Unbleached Titanium
1837 LEGACY	☐ Ecru S: Corn Silk H: White
OIL EQUIV.	☐ *WN White + Jaune Brillant 3:1

NOTES

T C S # OR-5-3-4

☐ *Peaches 'n Cream + Flesh Tone 1:1

☐ Island Coral
S: Desert Sun Orange H: Putty
☐ Peach Cobbler
S: Cinnamon H: Taffy
☐ *White + Gold Oxide 4:1

☐ Peachee
S: Cool Peach H: Corn Silk
☐ *WN White + Cadmium Yellow Pale + Bright
Red + Burnt Sienna 6:3:2:1

NOTES

BRAND	COLOR	COLOR

T C S # OR-5-5-3

AMERICANA	☐ *Moon Yellow + Flesh Tone 2:1
CERAMCOAT	☐ *Western Sunset + Fleshtone 1:1
FOLK ART	☐ *Skintone + Buttercrunch 2:1
JO SONJA	☐ *Warm White + Gold Oxide + Cadmium Yellow Light 5:2:1
1837 LEGACY	☐ Desert Tea S: Warm Beige H: Devon Cream
OIL EQUIV.	☐ *WN Cadmium Lemon + Jaune Brillant 2:1

NOTES

T C S # OR-5-7-3

	☐ *Sand + Flesh Tone 1:1
	☐ Dresden Flesh S: Light Chocolate H: Putty
	☐ *Almond Parfait + Georgia Peach 1:1
	☐ *Warm White + Provincial Beige 12:1 or Jo Sonja Bkg Cashmere
	☐ Ivory Cream S: Sandy Peach H: Corn Silk
	☐ *WN White + Raw Sienna + Cad. Red Light 12:6:1

NOTES

T C S # OR-5-9-3

AMERICANA	☐ *Flesh Tone + Antique White 1:1
CERAMCOAT	☐ *Dresden Flesh + Wild Rice 1:1
FOLK ART	☐ *Skintone + Linen 1:1
JO SONJA	☐ Skintone Base
1837 LEGACY	☐ *Skintone + Warm Beige 2:1
OIL EQUIV.	☐ *WN White + GRUM Burnt Sienna + WN Burnt Umber + Raw Sienna 12:2:1:1

NOTES

T C S # OR-5-9-6

	☐ *Peaches 'n Cream + Burnt Orange 3:1
	☐ Desert Sun Orange S: Burnt Sienna H: Rosetta
	☐ *Cinnamon + White 2:1
	☐ *Warm White + Gold Oxide 4:1
	☐ Salmon S: Pottery H: Corn Silk
	☐ *WN Burnt Sienna + White + REM Geranium Lake 3:2:1

NOTES

T C S # OR-5-9-7

AMERICANA	☐ *Burnt Orange + Medium Flesh 5:1
CERAMCOAT	☐ Santa Fe Rose S: Cinnamon H: Medium Flesh
FOLK ART	☐ Terra Cotta S: Buckskin Brown H: Peach Cobbler
JO SONJA	☐ *Warm White + Red Earth 2:1
1837 LEGACY	☐ Light Rose S: Red Iron Oxide H: Dusty Rose
OIL EQUIV.	☐ *WN Burnt Sienna + White + Bright Red 5:5:1

NOTES

T C S #OR-5-9-8

	☐ DeLane's Dark Flesh S: Brandy Wine H: Mocha
	☐ Cayenne S: Brown Iron Oxide H: Fleshtone
	☐ Cinnamon S: Burnt Sienna H: Georgia Peach
	☐ *Burnt Sienna + White 1:1 or Jo Sonja Bkg Rosehip
	☐ Red Pepper S: Brick H: Apricot
	☐ *WN Burnt Sienna + White + Alizarin Crimson 5:3:2

NOTES

BRAND **COLOR** **COLOR**

T C S # OR-6-3-1	**T C S #** OR-6-3-2

AMERICANA	☐ *White + Flesh Tone (T)	☐ *Flesh Tone + White 1:1
CERAMCOAT	☐ Santa's Flesh S: Normandy Rose H: White	☐ Santa's Flesh (L) S: Normandy Rose H: White
FOLK ART	☐ Georgia Peach S: Peach Perfection H: White	☐ *Georgia Peach + Skintone 6:1
JO SONJA	☐ *Warm White + Gold Oxide (T)	☐ *Warm White + Gold Oxide 14:1
1837 LEGACY	☐ *White + Natural Blush 8:1	☐ Corn Silk S: Natural Blush H: White
OIL EQUIV.	☐ *WN White + Bright Red + Cadmium Yellow Pale 20:1:2	☐ *WN White + Bright Red + Cadmium Yellow Pale 20:1:1
	NOTES	**NOTES**

T C S # OR-6-3-3	**T C S #** OR-6-3-4

AMERICANA	☐ *Flesh Tone + Medium Flesh 1:1	☐ Flesh Tone S: Sable Brown H: Hi-Lite Flesh
CERAMCOAT	☐ Peachy Keen S: Medium Flesh H: Queen Anne's Lace	☐ Fleshtone S: Desert Sun Orange H: Santa's Flesh
FOLK ART	☐ Skintone S: Cinnamon H: Portrait Light	☐ *Georgia Peach + Skintone 1:1
JO SONJA	☐ *Warm White + Gold Oxide 12:1	☐ *Warm White + Gold Oxide 8:1
1837 LEGACY	☐ Natural Blush S: Cool Peach H: Corn Silk	☐ Skin Tone S: Sandy Peach H: Corn Silk
OIL EQUIV.	☐ PRI Peach (Light Flesh)	☐ *WN White + Raw Sienna + Cadmium Red Light 12:4:1
	NOTES	**NOTES**

T C S # OR-6-3-5	**T C S #** OR-6-3-6

AMERICANA	☐ Medium Flesh S: Light Cinnamon H: Peaches 'n Cream	☐ *Medium Flesh + Burnt Orange 4:1
CERAMCOAT	☐ Medium Flesh S: Dark Flesh H: Fleshtone	☐ Caucasian Flesh S: Red Iron Oxide H: Fleshtone
FOLK ART	☐ *Skintone + Georgia Peach 2:1	☐ *Peach Cobbler + Cinnamon (T)
JO SONJA	☐ *Skin Tone Base + Norwegian Orange + Warm White 5:1:1	☐ *Jaune Brillant + Norwegian Orange 1:1
1837 LEGACY	☐ Medium Flesh S: Pottery H: Natural Blush	☐ Spiced Peach S: Red Iron Oxide H: Maiden's Blush
OIL EQUIV.	☐ *WN White+ Burnt Sienna + Bright Red 20:5:2	☐ *WN White + Burnt Sienna + REM Geranium Lake 3:2:1
	NOTES	**NOTES**

BRAND	COLOR	COLOR

T C S # OR-6-3-8

AMERICANA	Shading Flesh S: Light Cinnamon H: Base Flesh
CERAMCOAT	Dark Flesh S: Sonoma H: Rosetta
FOLK ART	*Cinnamon + Georgia Peach 3:1
JO SONJA	*Opal + Gold Oxide + Napthol Red Lt. 4:2:1
1837 LEGACY	Pottery S: Brick H: Natural Blush
OIL EQUIV.	*WN White + Burnt Sienna + Alizarin Crimson 5:5:1

NOTES

T C S # OR-6-7-2

AMERICANA	Base Flesh S: Shading Flesh H: Hi-Lite Flesh
CERAMCOAT	Normandy Rose (D) S: Sonoma Wine H: Dresden Flesh
FOLK ART	Portrait (AP) S: Cinnamon H: Georgia Peach
JO SONJA	*Opal + Burnt Sienna 10:1
1837 LEGACY	Sandy Peach S: Cashmere Rose H: Sea Shell Pink
OIL EQUIV.	*WN White + Burnt Sienna + Bright Red + French Ultramarine 20:10:2:1

NOTES

T C S # OR-6-7-3

AMERICANA	Dusty Rose S: Red Iron Oxide H: Dusty Rose + White 1:1
CERAMCOAT	Normandy Rose S: Sonoma Wine H: Dresden Flesh
FOLK ART	*Portrait + Victorian Rose 4:1
JO SONJA	*Opal + Burnt Sienna 8:1
1837 LEGACY	Opal S: Rose Dawn H: Cameo Pink
OIL EQUIV.	REM Barrick Flesh Medium

NOTES

T C S # OR-6-7-4

AMERICANA	*Cashmere Beige + Mauve 4:1
CERAMCOAT	Misty Mauve S: Rose Mist H: Pink Frosting
FOLK ART	*Portrait + Victorian Rose 4:1
JO SONJA	*Opal + Burnt Sienna 6:1
1837 LEGACY	Dusty Rose S: Light Rose H: Cameo Pink
OIL EQUIV.	REM Barrick Flesh Medium (L)

NOTES

T C S # RO-1-3-3

AMERICANA	*Peaches 'n Cream + Coral Rose + Burnt Orange 3:1:T
CERAMCOAT	*Medium Flesh + Caucasian Flesh 6:1
FOLK ART	*Promenade + Tangerine 2:1
JO SONJA	*White + Opal + Gold Oxide 3:2:1
1837 LEGACY	Apricot S: Spiced Peach H: Natural Blush
OIL EQUIV.	*WN Juane Brillant + Raw Sienna 4:1

NOTES

T C S # RO-2-3-3

AMERICANA	*Peaches N Cream + Dusty Rose (T)
CERAMCOAT	Rosetta Pink S: Adobe Pink H: Santa's Flesh
FOLK ART	Peach Perfection S: Cinnamon H: Georgia Peach
JO SONJA	*Warm White + Norwegian Orange 5:1
1837 LEGACY	Cherub S: Cashmere Rose H: Sea Shell Pink
OIL EQUIV.	*WN White + Burnt Sienna + Bright Red 10:5:1

NOTES

25

BRAND   **COLOR**   **COLOR**

T C S # RO-3-3-2

AMERICANA	☐ Soft Peach S: Peach Sherbet H: White
CERAMCOAT	☐ *Peachy Keen + Pink Frosting 3:1
FOLK ART	☐ *White + Bright Peach 2:1
JO SONJA	☐ *Unbleached Titanium + White + Vermillion 12:2:1
1837 LEGACY	☐ *Cameo Pink + Toast 4:1
OIL EQUIV.	☐ *WN White + Cadmium Yellow Deep + REM Cadmium Red Light 12:2:1

NOTES

T C S # RO-3-3-3

☐ Peaches 'n Cream S: Light Cinnamon H: Soft Peach
☐ *Pink Angel + White 6:1
☐ Bright Peach S: Salmon H: Georgia Peach
☐ *Warm White + Vermillion 5:1
☐ *Maiden's Blush + White 6:1
☐ *WN White + REM Geranium Lake + WN Cad. Yellow Medium 4:2:1

NOTES

T C S # RO-4-3-2

AMERICANA	☐ *Base Flesh + French Mauve 4:1
CERAMCOAT	☐ *Indiana Rose + Fleshtone 2:1
FOLK ART	☐ *Portrait + Spring Rose 4:1
JO SONJA	☐ *Opal + Rose Pink 12:1 Jo Sonja Bkg Blossom
1837 LEGACY	☐ *Skintone + Opal 4:1
OIL EQUIV.	☐ *WN White + GRUM Burnt Sienna + REM Cadmium Red Light 10:3:1

NOTES

T C S # RO-5-1-4

☐ *Cadmium Orange + Pumpkin 1:1
☐ *Tangerine + Pumpkin 1:1
☐ Pure Orange (AP) S: Burnt Sienna H: Tangerine
☐ Cadmium Orange
☐ *Fresh Tangerine + Duck Bill 1:1
☐ ARC Brilliant Orange, WN Winsor Orange

NOTES

T C S # RO-5-1-6

AMERICANA	☐ Tangelo Orange S: Oxblood H: Cadmium Yellow
CERAMCOAT	☐ Tangerine S: Red Iron Oxide H: Yellow
FOLK ART	☐ Autumn Leaves S: Light Red Oxide H: Taffy
JO SONJA	☐ *Vermillion + Yellow Light 4:1
1837 LEGACY	☐ Fresh Tangerine S: Russet H: Dandelion
OIL EQUIV.	☐ *WN Cadmium Yellow Pale + Bright Red + Burnt Sienna 4:2:1

NOTES

T C S # RO-5-1-7

☐ Cadmium Orange S: Georgia Clay H: Pumpkin
☐ Orange S: Tomato Spice H: Bittersweet
☐ Red Light (AP) S: Huckleberry H: White
☐ Vermillion
☐ Orange S: Red Iron Oxide H: Duck Bill
☐ ARC Superchrome Scarlet, PRI Cad. Red Light Hue, REM Geranium Lake, WN Scarlet Lake

NOTES

BRAND	COLOR	COLOR

T C S # RO-5-1-8

AMERICANA	☐ *Cadmium Orange + Cadmium Red 1:1
CERAMCOAT	☐ Poppy Orange S: Napthol Crimson H: Pumpkin
FOLK ART	☐ *Autumn Leaves + Calico Red 1:1
JO SONJA	☐ Vermillion (L)
1837 LEGACY	☐ *Fresh Tangerine + Napthol Crimson 1:1
OIL EQUIV.	☐ REM Cadmium Red Light, WN Winsor Red

NOTES

T C S # RO-5-2-5

☐ *Tangelo Orange + Burnt Orange 1:1

☐ *Georgia Clay + Terra Cotta 3:1

☐ *Pure Orange + Light Red Oxide 4:1

☐ *Norwegian Orange + Vermillion 3:1

☐ Russet
S: Red Iron Oxide H: Salmon
☐ *WN Cadmium Scarlet + Raw Sienna 3:1

NOTES

T C S # RO-5-3-1

AMERICANA	☐ *Flesh + Flesh Tone 8:1
CERAMCOAT	☐ *Santa's Flesh + Pink Frosting 1:1
FOLK ART	☐ Victorian Rose S: Cherokee Rose H: Warm White
JO SONJA	☐ *White + Norwegian Orange 15:1
1837 LEGACY	☐ *Cameo Pink + Corn Silk 2:1
OIL EQUIV.	☐ *WN White + Bright Red + Cadmium Yellow Pale 10:1:1

NOTES

T C S # RO-5-3-2

☐ *White + Gooseberry 3:1

☐ Indiana Rose
S: Antique Rose H: Pink Frosting
☐ *Victorian Rose + Promenade 2:1

☐ *Smoked Pearl + Rose Pink 4:1

☐ Damsel Rose
S: Rose Dawn H: Sea Shell Pink
☐ *WN White + Cad. Yellow Pale + Bright Red +
French Ultramarine. 12:3:2:1

NOTES

T C S # RO-5-3-3

AMERICANA	☐ *Dusty Rose + White 1:1
CERAMCOAT	☐ Pink Angel S: Adobe Pink H: Santa's Flesh
FOLK ART	☐ Promenade (D) S: Dark Brown H: Georgia Peach
JO SONJA	☐ *Warm White + Norwegian Orange (T)
1837 LEGACY	☐ Maiden's Blush S: Cashmere Rose H: Cameo Pink
OIL EQUIV.	☐ WN Flesh Tint

NOTES

T C S # RO-5-3-4

☐ Peach Sherbet
S: Gingerbread H: Soft Peach
☐ *Coral + Rosetta 1:1

☐ Promenade
S: Dark Brown H: Georgia Peach
☐ *Warm White + Norwegian Orange 4:1

☐ *Maiden's Blush + Cashmere Rose 6:1

☐ WN Rose Dore

NOTES

BRAND	COLOR		COLOR

T C S # RO-5-4-4

AMERICANA	☐ Burnt Orange (D) S: Burnt Sienna H: Cadmium Orange
CERAMCOAT	☐ Georgia Clay S: Red Iron Oxide H: Bittersweet
FOLK ART	☐ *Terra Cotta + Autumn Leaves 1:1
JO SONJA	☐ *Norwegian Orange + Vermillion 2:1
1837 LEGACY	☐ Burnt Clay S: Pumpkin Pie H: Duck Bill
OIL EQUIV.	☐ ARC Red Gold

NOTES

T C S # RO-5-4-5

AMERICANA	☐ Burnt Orange S: Burnt Sienna H: Cadmium Orange
CERAMCOAT	☐ *Georgia Clay + Burnt Sienna (T)
FOLK ART	☐ *Autumn Leaves + Cinnamon 3:1
JO SONJA	☐ *Norwegian Orange + Vermillion 3:1
1837 LEGACY	☐ Paprika S: Red Iron Oxide H: Burnt Clay
OIL EQUIV.	☐ WN Mars Orange

NOTES

T C S # RO-5-4-6

AMERICANA	☐ DeLane's Deep Shadow S: Brandy Wine H: Shading Flesh
CERAMCOAT	☐ *Cayenne + Red Iron Oxide 4:1
FOLK ART	☐ *Light Red Oxide + Autumn Leaves 4:1
JO SONJA	☐ *Norwegian Orange + Cadmium Orange 2:1
1837 LEGACY	☐ *Red Iron Oxide + Russet 1:1
OIL EQUIV.	☐ *GRUM Burnt Sienna + REM Cad. Red Light + White 2:1:1

NOTES

T C S # RO-5-4-7

AMERICANA	☐ Oxblood S: Antique Maroon H: Cadmium Orange
CERAMCOAT	☐ *Cayenne + Red Iron Oxide 3:1
FOLK ART	☐ *Autumn Leaves + Light Red Oxide 2:1
JO SONJA	☐ *Norwegian Orange + Burnt Sienna (T)
1837 LEGACY	☐ Brick S: Cinnabar H: Natural Blush
OIL EQUIV.	☐ REM Flesh Ochre, WN Terra Rosa

NOTES

T C S # RO-5-5-6

AMERICANA	☐ Gingerbread S: Heritage Brick H: Peach Sherbet
CERAMCOAT	☐ *Georgia Clay + Burnt Sienna + White 4:1:T
FOLK ART	☐ *Terra Cotta + Cinnamon 1:1
JO SONJA	☐ *Norwegian Orange + White + Burnt Sienna 10:10:1
1837 LEGACY	☐ *Russet + Bing Cherry + White 5:1:1
OIL EQUIV.	☐ *GRUM Bt. Sienna + REM Cad. Red Lt.+ WN Cad. Yellow Deep + White 4:4:1:1

NOTES

T C S # RO-7-4-7

AMERICANA	☐ Georgia Clay S: Antique Maroon H: Cadmium Orange
CERAMCOAT	☐ *Georgia Clay + Red Iron Oxide 1:1
FOLK ART	☐ *Red Light + Light Red Oxide 6:1
JO SONJA	☐ Norwegian Orange
1837 LEGACY	☐ Grit Red S: Red Iron Oxide H: Maiden's Blush
OIL EQUIV.	☐ ARC Light Red Oxide, *REM Geranium Lake + WN Burnt Sienna 3:1

NOTES

T C S # RO-8-3-4

AMERICANA	☐ Coral Rose S: Antique Rose H: Coral Rose + White 1:1
CERAMCOAT	☐ Coral S: Adobe Pink H: Queen Anne's Lace
FOLK ART	☐ *Salmon + Peach Perfection 6:1
JO SONJA	☐ *Warm White + Rose Pink 3:1
1837 LEGACY	☐ Cashmere Rose S: Festive Pink H: Maiden's Blush
OIL EQUIV.	☐ REM Barrick Flesh Blush

NOTES

T C S # RO-8-3-5

☐ Coral Rose (L) S: Antique Rose H: Coral Rose + White 1:1
☐ Coral (L) S: Adobe Pink H: Queen Anne's Lace
☐ Salmon S: Light Red Oxide H: White
☐ *Warm White + Rose Pink 2:1
☐ Cashmere Rose (L) S: Festive Pink H: Maiden's Blush
☐ *WN White + Bright Red + Cadmium Yellow Pale + French Ultramarine 16:4:4:1

NOTES

T C S # RO-8-3-6

AMERICANA	☐ DeLane's Cheek Color S: Country Red H: Coral Rose
CERAMCOAT	☐ Adobe Red (D) S: Red Iron Oxide H: Coral
FOLK ART	☐ *Salmon + Cinnamon 7:1
JO SONJA	☐ *Norwegian Orange + Rose Pink 3:1
1837 LEGACY	☐ *Red Iron Oxide + Festive Pink 1:1
OIL EQUIV.	☐ *REM Cadmium Red Light + Alizarin Crimson + White 3:1:1

NOTES

T C S # RO-8-3-7

☐ Antique Rose S: Tomato Red H: Coral Rose
☐ Adobe Red S: Red Iron Oxide H: Coral
☐ *Salmon + Cinnamon 6:1
☐ *Warm White + Rose Pink + Gold Oxide 1:1:1
☐ *Cashmere Rose + Red Iron Oxide 1:1
☐ *WN Cadmium Red Medium + Raw Sienna + White 2:2:1

NOTES

T C S # RE-3-2-2

AMERICANA	☐ *Spice Pink + Flesh Tone 1:1
CERAMCOAT	☐ *Indiana Rose + Pink Frosting 1:1
FOLK ART	☐ *White + Strawberry Parfait 3:1
JO SONJA	☐ *Opal + Rose Pink (T)
1837 LEGACY	☐ Wild Rose S: Peony Pink H: White
OIL EQUIV.	☐ *WN White + Bright Red + Cadmium Yellow Pale 2:1:1

NOTES

T C S # RE-3-2-4

☐ *Coral Reef + White 1:1
☐ Nector Coral S: Gypsy Rose H: Pink Frosting
☐ *Georgia Peach + Strawberry Parfait 2:1
☐ *Warm White + Norwegian Orange + Rose Pink 4:1:T
☐ Rouge S: Cashmere Rose H: Sea Shell Pink
☐ *WN Bright Red + Cadmium Yellow Pale + White 1:1:1

NOTES

BRAND   COLOR   COLOR

T C S # RE-3-2-5

AMERICANA	☐ Blush Flesh (D) S: Country Red H: Coral Rose
CERAMCOAT	☐ Fiesta Pink S: Rouge H: Nector Coral
FOLK ART	☐ *Poppy Red + Salmon 2:1
JO SONJA	☐ *Vermillion + Opal 3:1
1837 LEGACY	☐ Festive Pink S: Brick H: Rouge
OIL EQUIV.	☐ *WN Cadmium Red Medium + White + Raw Sienna 4:3:1

NOTES

T C S # RE-3-2-6

☐ Blush Flesh   S: Country Red H: Coral Rose
☐ Persimmon   S: Rouge H: Pink Angel
☐ Poppy Red   S: Huckleberry H: Tapioca
☐ *Rose Pink + Vermillion + Jaune Brillant 3:1:1
☐ Autumn Leaf (D)   S: Bing Cherry H: Maiden's Blush
☐ PRI Prima Pink

NOTES

T C S # RE-3-2-7

AMERICANA	☐ Blush Flesh (L) S: Country Red H: Coral Rose
CERAMCOAT	☐ Rouge S: Red Iron Oxide H: Nector Coral
FOLK ART	☐ *Poppy Red + Christmas Red 4:1
JO SONJA	☐ *Vermillion + Rose Pink 1:1
1837 LEGACY	☐ Autumn Leaf S: Bing Cherry H: Maiden's Blush
OIL EQUIV.	☐ *WN Cadmium Red Medium + Yellow Ochre 2:1

NOTES

T C S # RE-3-5-3

☐ *Flesh Tone + Coral Rose 3:1
☐ *Santa's Flesh + Nectar 2:1
☐ *Georgia Peach + Sweetheart Pink 2:1
☐ *White + Rose Pink +   Cadmium Yellow Light 8:2:1
☐ Peony Pink   S: Cashmere Rose H: Sea Shell Pink
☐ *WN White + REM Cadmium Red Light 5:1

NOTES

T C S # RE-3-5-5

AMERICANA	☐ Gooseberry Pink S: Crimson Tide H: HiLite Flesh
CERAMCOAT	☐ Antique Rose S: Burgundy Rose H: Pink Frosting
FOLK ART	☐ * Potpourri Rose + Peach Perfection 5:1
JO SONJA	☐ *Opal + Plum Pink + Rose Pink 7:1:1
1837 LEGACY	☐ Madder Rose S: Grecian Rose H: Faded Rose
OIL EQUIV.	☐ *WN White + Alizarin Crimson + Burnt Umber + Cadmium Yellow Pale 4:1:1:1

NOTES

T C S # RE-3-5-7

☐ *Gooseberry Pink + Brandy Wine 1:1
☐ Gypsy Rose   S: Burgundy Rose H: Pink Frosting
☐ *Rose Garden + Promenade 1:1
☐ *Warm White + Rose Pink + Gold Oxide 2:2:1
☐ Rose Dawn   S: Red Iron Oxide H: Peony Pink
☐ *WN Bright Red + Raw Sienna + White 3:2:1

NOTES

TCS #RE-4-1-5

AMERICANA	☐ Cadmium Red S: Crimson Tide H: Pumpkin
CERAMCOAT	☐ *Napthol Crimson + Orange 1:1
FOLK ART	☐ *Christmas Red + Red Light 3:1
JO SONJA	☐ Cadmium Scarlet Jo Sonja Bkg Holiday Red
1837 LEGACY	☐ Persian Red S: Valentine Red H: Orange
OIL EQUIV.	☐ ARC Cadmium Scarlet

NOTES

TCS #RE-4-1-6

☐ Brilliant Red
S: Deep Burgundy H: Tangelo Orange
☐ *Bright Red + Napthol Crimson 1:1
☐ *Red Light + Napthol Crimson 1:1
☐ Napthol Red Light
☐ Coronado Red
S: Napthol Red Light H: Orange
☐ ARC Napthol Scarlet,
WN Vermilion Hue

NOTES

TCS #RE-4-2-5

AMERICANA	☐ Country Red S: Antique Maroon H: Antique Rose
CERAMCOAT	☐ Tomato Spice (D) S: Candy Bar Brown H: Fiesta Pink
FOLK ART	☐ *Red Light + Apple Spice 2:1
JO SONJA	☐ *Napthol Red Light + Raw Umber 8:1
1837 LEGACY	☐ Bing Cherry S: Sumac Red H: Persian Red
OIL EQUIV.	☐ *WN Bright Red + Purple Lake 4:1

NOTES

TCS #RE-4-2-6

☐ Tomato Red
S: Napa Red H: Cadmium Red
☐ Tomato Spice
S: Candy Bar Brown H: Fiesta Pink
☐ *Red Light + Apple Spice 1:1
☐ *Napthol Red Light + Raw Umber 5:1
☐ Ripe Tomato
S: Cinnabar H: Rouge
☐ *WN Bright Red + Yellow Ochre 4:1

NOTES

TCS #RE-4-2-7

AMERICANA	☐ Crimson Tide S: Black Plum H: Brilliant Red
CERAMCOAT	☐ Moroccan Red S: Sonoma Wine H: Poppy Orange
FOLK ART	☐ Barnyard Red S: Burnt Umber H: Georgia Peach
JO SONJA	☐ *Rose Pink + Burgundy 3:1
1837 LEGACY	☐ Sumac Red S: Cinnabar H: Fire Truck Red
OIL EQUIV.	☐ ARC Permanent Brown Madder

NOTES

TCS #RE-4-3-1

☐ Hi-Lite Flesh
S: Base Flesh H: White
☐ Pink Frosting
S: Hydrangea H: White
☐ Cotton Candy
S: Rose Chiffon H: White
☐ *Warm White + Rose Pink (T)
☐ Cameo Pink
S: Peony Pink H: White
☐ *WN White + Alizarin Crimson +
Burnt Umber 20:1:1

NOTES

BRAND   **COLOR**   **COLOR**

T C S # RE-4-3-3

AMERICANA	☐ *Spice Pink + White 2:1
CERAMCOAT	☐ *Nector Coral + White 1:1
FOLK ART	☐ Sweetheart Pink (D) S: Raspberry Sherbert H: White
JO SONJA	☐ *White + Napthol Red Light 3:1
1837 LEGACY	☐ Sea Shell Pink S: Rouge H: Cameo Pink
OIL EQUIV.	☐ *WN White + REM Cad. Red Lt. + WN Yellow Ochre 8:2:1

NOTES

T C S # RE-4-3-4

☐ *Spice Pink + White 1:1
☐ *Nectar Coral + Lisa Pink 1:1
☐ Sweetheart Pink S: Raspberry Sherbert H: White
☐ *White + Napthol Crimson 10:1
☐ *Daybreak + Sea Shell Pink 1:1
☐ *WN White + Bright Red + Cadmium Yellow Pale 16:2:1

NOTES

T C S # RE-4-3-5

AMERICANA	☐ Spice Pink S: Antique Rose H: Spice Pink + White 1:1
CERAMCOAT	☐ *Deep Coral + White 2:1
FOLK ART	☐ *Primrose + Strawberry Parfait 1:1
JO SONJA	☐ *White + Rose Pink 3:1
1837 LEGACY	☐ *Maiden's Blush + Geranium Red 3:1
OIL EQUIV.	☐ *WN White + Bright Red + Cadmium Yellow Medium 4:2:1

NOTES

T C S # RE-4-3-6

☐ *Coral Rose + Spice Pink 1:1
☐ *Coral + Pretty Pink 2:1
☐ Strawberry Parfait S: Rose Garden H: Victorian Rose
☐ *Warm White + Rose Pink 4:1
☐ *Cashmere Rose + Hot Pink 2:1
☐ WN Rose Madder Genuine

NOTES

T C S # RE-4-3-7

AMERICANA	☐ *Crimson + Brandy Wine 2:1
CERAMCOAT	☐ *Maroon + Candy Bar Brown 4:1
FOLK ART	☐ *Lipstick + Apple Spice 2:1
JO SONJA	☐ Brown Madder
1837 LEGACY	☐ Wild Berry S: Burgundy H: Fire Truck Red
OIL EQUIV.	☐ REM Brownish Madder (Alizarin)

NOTES

T C S # RE-4-3-8

☐ *Boysenberry + Crimson Tide 3:1
☐ Deep Coral S: Burgundy Rose H: Hydrangea
☐ Primrose S: Maroon H: Portrait
☐ Rose Pink
☐ *Ripe Tomato + Carnation Pink 2:1
☐ WN Rose Madder Deep

NOTES

T C S # RE-4-4-3

AMERICANA	☐ *White + Mauve 4:1
CERAMCOAT	☐ Rose Cloud S: Rose Mist H: Pink Frosting
FOLK ART	☐ *Berries 'n Cream + Victorian Rose 3:1
JO SONJA	☐ *Opal + Plum Pink 5:1
1837 LEGACY	☐ Faded Rose S: Rose Dawn H: Wild Rose
OIL EQUIV.	☐ REM Rose Madder Antique, *WN White + Bright Red + Raw Sienna 4:2:1

NOTES

T C S # RE-4-4-5

	☐ *Gooseberry Pink + Antique Mauve 4:1
	☐ *Antique Rose + Sachet 1:1
	☐ Rose Chiffon S: Raspberry Wine H: Cotton Candy
	☐ *Opal + Plum Pink + Indian Red Oxide 5:1:T
	☐ *Madder Rose + Lupin Pink 1:1
	☐ *WN White + Alizarin Crimson + Burnt Umber + Cadmium Yellow Pale 8:1:1:1

NOTES

T C S # RE-4-6-5

AMERICANA	☐ Red Iron Oxide S: Antique Maroon H: Burnt Orange
CERAMCOAT	☐ Red Iron Oxide S: Candy Bar Brown H: Coral
FOLK ART	☐ Light Red Oxide (AP) S: Burnt Sienna H: Taffy
JO SONJA	☐ Red Earth Jo Sonja Bkg Spice
1837 LEGACY	☐ Red Iron Oxide S: Cinnabar H: Burnt Clay
OIL EQUIV.	☐ WN Indian Red

NOTES

T C S # RE-4-6-7

	☐ Heritage Brick S: Black Plum H: Antique Rose
	☐ *Burgundy Rose + Red Iron Oxide 2:1
	☐ Apple Spice S: Raspberry Wine H: Victorian Rose
	☐ *Red Earth + Burgundy 1:1
	☐ *Burgundy + Red Iron Oxide 2:1
	☐ WN Mars Violet

NOTES

T C S # RE-4-6-8

AMERICANA	☐ Brandy Wine S: Antique Maroon H: Antique Rose
CERAMCOAT	☐ Burgundy Rose S: Midnight H: Antique Rose
FOLK ART	☐ Huckleberry S: Dark Brown H: Cotton Candy
JO SONJA	☐ *Norwegian Orange + Indian Red Oxide 4:1
1837 LEGACY	☐ *Burgundy + Cinnabar 2:1
OIL EQUIV.	☐ *WN Venetian Red + Alizarin Crimson + Burnt Umber 2:2:1

NOTES

T C S # RE-5-1-1

	☐ *White + Flesh 2:1
	☐ *White + Napthol Red Light 15:1
	☐ Portrait Light S: Portrait H: White
	☐ *Warm White + Napthol Crimson 12:1
	☐ *White + Napthol Red Light 15:1
	☐ *WN White + Cadmium Yellow Pale + Bright Red 40:1:1

NOTES

BRAND	COLOR	COLOR

T C S #RE-5-1-4

AMERICANA ☐ Calico Red
S: Deep Burgundy H: Blush

CERAMCOAT ☐ Opaque Red
S: Black Cherry H: Red Orange

FOLK ART ☐ *Christmas Red + Red Light 1:1

JO SONJA ☐ *Napthol Red Light + Napthol Crimson 3:1

1837 LEGACY ☐ *Napthol Crimson + Geranium Red 6:1

OIL EQUIV. ☐ WN Bright Red

NOTES

T C S # RE-5-1-5

☐ Napthol Red
S: Napa Red H: Blush

☐ Napthol Crimson
S: Black Cherry H: Tangerine

☐ Christmas Red
S: Raspberry Wine H: Tapioca

☐ *Cadmium Scarlet + Napthol Crimson (T)

☐ Napthol Crimson (D)
S: Sumac Red H: Orange

☐ *WN Bright Red + Scarlet Lake 1:1

NOTES

T C S #RE-5-1-6

AMERICANA ☐ Cherry Red
S: Napa Red H: Blush

CERAMCOAT ☐ Bright Red
S: Black Cherry H: Tangerine

FOLK ART ☐ Lipstick Red
S: Alizarin Crimson H: Red Light

JO SONJA ☐ *Napthol Red Light + Napthol Crimson 1:1

1837 LEGACY ☐ Napthol Crimson
S: Sumac Red H: Orange

OIL EQUIV. ☐ ARC Archival Crimson,
PRI Cadmium Red Medium Hue,
WN Winsor Red Deep

NOTES

T C S # RE-5-2-5

☐ *Baby Pink + Calico Red 2:1

☐ Pretty Pink
S: Berry Red H: Pink Frosting

☐ *White + Hot Pink + Poppy Red 2:2:1

☐ *White + Napthol Crimson +
Trans. Magenta 2:1:T

☐ *Geranium Red + White 2:1

☐ No Oil assignment

NOTES

This color is difficult to
match because of its
flourescent qualities.

T C S #RE-5-3-5

AMERICANA ☐ *Antique Rose + Cadmium Red 1:1

CERAMCOAT ☐ Fruit Punch
S: Moroccan Red H: Tangerine

FOLK ART ☐ *Christmas Red + Strawberry Parfait 6:1

JO SONJA ☐ *Napthol Red Light + Rose Pink 1:1

1837 LEGACY ☐ *Napthol Crimson + Persian Red 1:1

OIL EQUIV. ☐ *WN Cadmium Red Light + Bright Red +
White 6:2:1

NOTES

T C S #RE-5-5-8

☐ Antique Maroon
S: Black Plum H: Santa Red

☐ Candy Bar Brown
S: Black H: Gypsy Rose

☐ *Apple Spice + Huckleberry 3:1

☐ *Burgundy + Indian Red Oxide 6:1

☐ Cinnabar
S: Velvet Night H: Rose Dawn

☐ WN Mars Violet Deep

NOTES

| BRAND | COLOR | COLOR |

T C S # RE-5-6-9

BRAND	
AMERICANA	☐ Rookwood Red S: Black Plum H: Cherry Red
CERAMCOAT	☐ Sonoma Wine S: Black H: Gypsy Rose
FOLK ART	☐ *Huckleberry + Burnt Sienna 1:1
JO SONJA	☐ Indian Red Oxide Jo Sonja Bkg Deep Plum
1837 LEGACY	☐ Black Ruby S: Velvet Night H: Winter Wine
OIL EQUIV.	☐ ARC Transparent Red Oxide, REM Permanent Brown Madder

NOTES

T C S # RE-5-8-5

☐ French Mocha
  S: Antique Maroon H: Warm Neutral
☐ *Dark Flesh + Cinnamon 3:1

☐ *Teddy Bear Brown + Potpourri Rose 2:1

☐ *Burnt Sienna + Smoked Pearl +
  Indian Red Oxide 2:2:1
☐ *Light Rose + Nutmeg 6:1

☐ *WN White + REM Alizarin Crimson + WN
  Burnt Umber + GRUM Bt. Sienna 8:2:1:1

NOTES

T C S # RE-6-1-5

BRAND	
AMERICANA	☐ True Red S: Rookwood Red H: Cadmium Orange
CERAMCOAT	☐ Fire Red S: Mendocino Red H: Pumpkin
FOLK ART	☐ *Christmas Red + Calico Red 1:1
JO SONJA	☐ *Napthol Red Light + Napthol Crimson 2:1
1837 LEGACY	☐ Fire Truck Red S: Pthalo Crimson H: Orange
OIL EQUIV.	☐ *WN Bright Red + White 6:1

NOTES

T C S # RE-6-1-6

☐ Berry Red
  S: Napa Red H: Cadmium Red
☐ Cardinal Red
  S: Black Cherry H: Tangerine
☐ Engine Red
  S: Alizarin Crimson H: Red Light
☐ *Napthol Crimson + Napthol Red Light 1:1

☐ Mountie Red
  S: Sumac Red H: Orange
☐ *WN Bright Red + Alizarin Crimson +
  White 5:3:2

NOTES

T C S # RE-6-2-1

BRAND	
AMERICANA	☐ *White + Spice Pink (T)
CERAMCOAT	☐ Seashell White S: Hydrangea Pink H: White
FOLK ART	☐ Rose White S: Baby Pink H: White
JO SONJA	☐ *White + Napthol Red Crimson (T)
1837 LEGACY	☐ *White + Carnation Pink (T)
OIL EQUIV.	☐ *WN White + Alizarin Crimson + Burnt Umber 50:1:1

NOTES

T C S # RE-6-2-3

☐ *White + Spice Pink 3:1

☐ Hydrangea Pink
  S: Fuchsia H: Pink Frosting
☐ *White + Calico Red 7:1

☐ *White + Napthol Red Light 7:1

☐ Carnation Pink
  S: Daybreak H: Wild Rose
☐ *WN White + Bright Red + Alizarin Crimson +
  Raw Sienna 6:2:1:1

NOTES

35

BRAND   **COLOR**   **COLOR**

T C S # RE-6-2-4

AMERICANA   ☐ *Baby Pink + Spice Pink (T)

CERAMCOAT   ☐ Lisa Pink
                S: Mendocino Red H: Pink Frosting

FOLK ART   ☐ *White + Calico Red 4:1

JO SONJA   ☐ *White + Napthol Red Light 4:1

1837 LEGACY ☐ Daybreak
                S: Winter Wine H: Wild Rose

OIL EQUIV.   ☐ *WN White + Bright Red + Alizarin Crimson +
                Raw Sienna 4:2:2:1

NOTES

T C S # RE-6-2-6

☐ Primary Red
   S: Napa Red H: Tangelo Orange
☐ Napthol Red Light
   S: Black Cherry H: Tangerine
☐ Calico Red
   S: Raspberry Wine H: Pure Orange
☐ Napthol Crimson (D)

☐ Napthol Red Light
   S: Cranberry H: Geranium Red
☐ WN Cadmium Red

NOTES

T C S # RE-6-2-7

AMERICANA   ☐ Santa Red
                S: Napa Red H: Cadmium Red

CERAMCOAT   ☐ Tompte Red
                S: Black Cherry H: Hydrangea

FOLK ART   ☐ Napthol Crimson (AP) (D)
                S: Alizarin Crimson H: Baby Pink

JO SONJA   ☐ Napthol Crimson

1837 LEGACY ☐ *Pthalo Crimson + Napthol Red Light 1:1

OIL EQUIV.   ☐ ARC Cadmium Red Mid,
                REM Rembrandt Rose,
                WN Carmine

NOTES

T C S # RE-6-2-8

☐ *Country Red + Berry Red 1:1

☐ Tompte Red (L)
   S: Black Cherry H: Hydrangea
☐ Napthol Crimson (AP)
   S: Alizarin Crimson H: Baby Pink
☐ Napthol Crimson (L)
   Jo Sonja Bkg Victorian Red
☐ Pthalo Crimson
   S: Cranberry H: Mountie Red
☐ ARC Napthol Crimson,
   WN Cadmium Red Deep

NOTES

T C S # RE-6-3-2

AMERICANA   ☐ Baby Pink
                S: Royal Fuchsia H: Pink Chiffon

CERAMCOAT   ☐ *Hydrangea + Fuchsia (T)

FOLK ART   ☐ Baby Pink
                S: Pink H: White

JO SONJA   ☐ *White + Napthol Crimson 6:1

1837 LEGACY ☐ *White + Geranium Red 4:1

OIL EQUIV.   ☐ *WN White + Bright Red +
                Alizarin Crimson 4:1:1

NOTES

T C S # RE-6-4-3

☐ Peony Pink
   S: Alizarin Crimson H: Spice Pink
☐ *Crimson + White 1:1

☐ Bright Pink
   S: Alizarin Crimson H: Sweetheart Pink
☐ *White + Napthol Crimson 2:1

☐ *White + Napthol Red Light 1:1

☐ *WN White + GRUM Thalo Red Rose +
   REM Cad. Red Lt. 2:2:1

NOTES

T C S # RE-6-4-4

AMERICANA
- ☐ *Calico Red + Crimson Tide (T)

CERAMCOAT
- ☐ Crimson
  S: Mendocino Red H: Hydrangea

FOLK ART
- ☐ Cardinal Red
  S: Maroon H: White

JO SONJA
- ☐ *Napthol Crimson + Rose Pink 2:1

1837 LEGACY
- ☐ Valentine
  S: Burgundy H: Daybreak

OIL EQUIV.
- ☐ REM ACRA Red

NOTES

T C S # RE-6-4-5

- ☐ Alizarin Crimson
  S: Cranberry Wine H: Cherry Red
- ☐ *Maroon + Berry Red 1:1

- ☐ Holiday Red
  S: Raspberry Wine H: Baby Pink
- ☐ *Rose Pink + Burgundy 5:1

- ☐ *Raspberry + Geranium Red 1:1

- ☐ *WN Bright Red + Alizarin Crimson + Burnt
  Umber + White 2:3:1:1

NOTES

T C S # RE-6-4-7

AMERICANA
- ☐ Burgundy Wine (D)
  S: Cranberry Wine H: Peony Pink

CERAMCOAT
- ☐ Maroon
  S: Candy Bar Brown H: Lisa Pink

FOLK ART
- ☐ Burgundy
  S: Raspberry Wine H: Pink

JO SONJA
- ☐ *Napthol Red Light + Burgundy 2:1

1837 LEGACY
- ☐ Raspberry
  S: Burgundy H: Daybreak

OIL EQUIV.
- ☐ *WN Aliz. Crim. + Bright Red + Burnt Umber +
  French Ultramarine. + White 3:1:1:1:1

NOTES

T C S # RE-6-4-8

- ☐ Burgundy Wine
  S: Cranberry Wine H: Peony Pink
- ☐ Black Cherry
  S: Candy Bar Brown H: Berry Red
- ☐ Alizarin Crimson (AP)
  S: True Burgundy H: Pink
- ☐ Permanent Alizarin

- ☐ Cranberry
  S: Cinnabar H: Daybreak
- ☐ ARC Indian Red,
  PRI Alizarin Crimson,
  REM Madder Lake

NOTES

T C S # RE-6-4-9

AMERICANA
- ☐ Deep Burgundy
  S: Black Plum H: Cherry Red

CERAMCOAT
- ☐ Barn Red
  S: Burgundy Rose H: Wild Rose

FOLK ART
- ☐ True Burgundy (AP)
  S: Navy Blue H: Berries 'n Cream

JO SONJA
- ☐ Burgundy

1837 LEGACY
- ☐ Burgundy
  S: Velvet Night H: Napthol Crimson

OIL EQUIV.
- ☐ ARC Permanent Alizarin,
  REM Alizarin Crimson

NOTES

T C S # RE-6-5-1

- ☐ Pink Chiffon
  S: Baby Pink H: White
- ☐ Rose Petal Pink
  S: Hydrangea H: White
- ☐ *White + Ballet Pink 1:1

- ☐ *Warm White + Rose Pink 16:1

- ☐ *White + Winter Wine 15:1

- ☐ *WN White + Bright Red +
  Alizarin Crimson 10:1:1

NOTES

BRAND   **COLOR**   **COLOR**

RED 6-5-2 / RED 6-5-8

T C S # RE-6-5-2

- AMERICANA: ☐ *White + Raspberry 4:1
- CERAMCOAT: ☐ *Pink Quartz + White 2:1
- FOLK ART: ☐ Ballet Pink
  S: Rose Crimson H: Rose White
- JO SONJA: ☐ *Opal + Rose Pink 12:1
- 1837 LEGACY: ☐ *White + Daybreak + Soft Lilac 6:1:T
- OIL EQUIV.: ☐ *WN White + Alizarin Crimson + Burnt Umber 24:1:1

NOTES

T C S # RE-6-5-3

- ☐ *White + Raspberry 3:1
- ☐ Pink Quartz
  S: Black Cherry H: Pink Frosting
- ☐ *Raspberry Sherbert + White 1:1
- ☐ *Opal + Plum Pink 10:1
- ☐ *Daybreak + Soft Lilac 3:1
- ☐ *WN White + Bright Red + Alizarin Crimson 4:2:1

NOTES

T C S # RE-6-5-4

- AMERICANA: ☐ *Raspberry + White 1:1
- CERAMCOAT: ☐ *Pink Quartz + Dusty Mauve 4:1
- FOLK ART: ☐ Rose Pink
  S: Maroon H: Spring Rose
- JO SONJA: ☐ *Opal + Plum Pink 7:1
- 1837 LEGACY: ☐ *Winter Wine + Burgundy 4:1
- OIL EQUIV.: ☐ *WN White + Alizarin Crimson + Burnt Umber 4:1:1

NOTES

T C S # RE-6-5-5

- ☐ Raspberry
  S: Cranberry Wine H: Spice Pink
- ☐ Wild Rose
  S: Barn Red H: Rose Cloud
- ☐ Raspberry Sherbert
  S: Maroon H: Sweetheart Pink
- ☐ *Opal + Plum Pink 1:1
- ☐ *Winter Wine + Burgundy 3:1
- ☐ *WN White + Bright Red + Alizarin Crimson + Burnt Umber 10:3:2:1

NOTES

T C S # RE-6-5-7

- AMERICANA: ☐ Antique Mauve
  S: Rookwood Red H: Mauve
- CERAMCOAT: ☐ Dusty Mauve
  S: Sonoma H: Rose Cloud
- FOLK ART: ☐ Rose Garden
  S: Raspberry Wine H: Spring Rose
- JO SONJA: ☐ Plum Pink
- 1837 LEGACY: ☐ Winter Wine
  S: Burgundy H: Lupin Pink
- OIL EQUIV.: ☐ *WN Bright Red + Alizarin Crimson + Burnt Umber + White 3:1:3:5

NOTES

T C S # RE-6-5-8

- ☐ Cranberry Wine
  S: Black Plum H: Boysenberry
- ☐ *Black Cherry + Burgundy Rose (T)
- ☐ Maroon
  S: Licorice H: Baby Pink
- ☐ *Plum Pink + Burgundy 3:1
- ☐ *Cranberry + Burgundy (T)
- ☐ ARC Mars Violet

NOTES

38

BRAND	COLOR	COLOR

T C S # RE-6-7-2

AMERICANA	☐ *White + Mauve 3:1
CERAMCOAT	☐ *Sachet + White 1:1
FOLK ART	☐ Spring Rose S: Rose Garden H: White
JO SONJA	☐ *Opal + Plum Pink 6:1
1837 LEGACY	☐ *Lupin Pink + White 1:1
OIL EQUIV.	☐ *WN White + Alizarin Crimson + Burnt Umber 12:1:1

NOTES

T C S #RE-6-7-4

AMERICANA	☐ French Mauve S: Antique Mauve H: Pink Chiffon
CERAMCOAT	☐ Sachet Pink S: Rose Mist H: Pink Frosting
FOLK ART	☐ Berries 'n Cream S: Rose Garden H: Cotton Candy
JO SONJA	☐ *Opal + Plum Pink 3:1
1837 LEGACY	☐ Lupin Pink S: Potpourri Rose H: Wild Rose
OIL EQUIV.	☐ *WN White + Alizarin Crimson + Burnt Umber 6:1:1

NOTES

T C S # RE-6-7-5

AMERICANA	☐ Mauve S: Cranberry Wine H: French Mauve
CERAMCOAT	☐ Bouquet Pink S: Sonoma H: Rose Cloud
FOLK ART	☐ Potpourri Rose S: Raspberry Wine H: Portrait Light
JO SONJA	☐ *Opal + Plum Pink 2:1
1837 LEGACY	☐ Potpourri Rose S: Grecian Rose H: Wild Rose
OIL EQUIV.	☐ *WN White + Alizarin Crimson + Burnt Umber + French Ultramarine 5:1:1:1

NOTES

T C S # RE-6-7-7

AMERICANA	☐ *Mauve + Cranberry Wine 2:1
CERAMCOAT	☐ Rose Mist S: Sonoma H: Sachet
FOLK ART	☐ *Rose Garden + Potpourri Rose 1:1
JO SONJA	☐ *Plum Pink + Indian Red Oxide 4:1 Jo Sonja Bkg Damask Rose
1837 LEGACY	☐ Grecian Rose S: Burgundy H: Lupin Pink
OIL EQUIV.	☐ *WN White + Burnt Umber + Bright Red 3:2:1

NOTES

T C S # RE-6-8-4

AMERICANA	☐ *Mauve + French Mauve 1:1
CERAMCOAT	☐ *Sachet + Misty Mauve 2:1
FOLK ART	☐ *Berries 'n Cream + Potpourri Rose 1:1
JO SONJA	☐ *Opal + Plum Pink 10:1
1837 LEGACY	☐ Terra Rosa S: Potpourri Rose H: Carnation Pink
OIL EQUIV.	☐ *WN White + Burnt Umber + REM Alizarin Crimson + WN Yellow Ochre 14:3:2:1

NOTES

T C S # RE-7-2-5

AMERICANA	☐ *True Red + Boysenberry Pink 1:1
CERAMCOAT	☐ Berry Red S: Black Cherry H: Hydrangea
FOLK ART	☐ *Cardinal Red + Pink (T)
JO SONJA	☐ *Napthol Crimson + Trans. Magenta 1:1
1837 LEGACY	☐ Geranium Red S: Cranberry H: Daybreak
OIL EQUIV.	☐ *WN Bright Red + White 3:1

NOTES

BRAND	COLOR	COLOR

T C S # RE-7-2-9

AMERICANA ☐ Black Plum
S: Soft Black H: Plum

CERAMCOAT ☐ Chocolate Cherry
S: Black H: Tompte Red

FOLK ART ☐ Burnt Carmine (AP)
S: Pure Black H: Napthol Crimson

JO SONJA ☐ Purple Madder

1837 LEGACY ☐ *Geranium Red + Cinnabar 3:1

OIL EQUIV. ☐ ARC Purple Madder,
REM Burnt Carmine,
WN Purple Lake

NOTES

T C S # RE-7-6-4

☐ *Boysenberry Pink + White 2:1

☐ Pink Parfait
S: Wild Rose H: Pink Frosting
☐ Pink
S: Rose Garden H: White
☐ *White + Napthol Crimson 4:1

☐ *Geranium Red + Lupin Pink 1:1

☐ *WN Bright Red + Alizarin Crimson + White +
Cadmium Yellow Pale 2:1:8:1

NOTES

T C S # RE-7-6-5

AMERICANA ☐ *Boysenberry Pink + True Red 3:1

CERAMCOAT ☐ *Pretty Pink + Berry Red 1:1

FOLK ART ☐ Hot Pink
S: Maroon H: Baby Pink

JO SONJA ☐ *White + Napthol Crimson 2:1

1837 LEGACY ☐ *Geranium Red + Winter Wine 3:1

OIL EQUIV. ☐ *WN Permanent Rose + White +
Cadmium Yellow Pale 4:2:1

NOTES

T C S # RV-1-2-5

☐ Boysenberry Pink
S: Country Red H: Spice Pink
☐ Fuchsia
S: Mendocino Red H: Hydrangea
☐ *Alizarin Crimson + White 2:1

☐ *Trans. Magenta + White 2:1

☐ *Geranium Red + Daybreak 3:1

☐ WN Permanent Rose

NOTES

T C S # RV-1-2-6

AMERICANA ☐ Royal Fuchsia
S: Red Violet H: Spice Pink

CERAMCOAT ☐ Fuchsia (L)
S: Mendocino Red H: Hydrangea Pink

FOLK ART ☐ Magenta
S: Raspberry Wine H: Baby Pink

JO SONJA ☐ Red Violet

1837 LEGACY ☐ *Geranium Red + Daybreak 2:1

OIL EQUIV. ☐ *WN Perm. Rose + Aliz. Crim. + Burnt Umber +
White + Ultramarine 16:2:1:2 :1

NOTES

T C S # RV-1-2-7

☐ *Burgundy Wine + Blue Violet (T)

☐ Sweetheart Blush
S: Candy Bar Brown H: Fuchsia
☐ Raspberry Wine
S: Licorice H: Potpourri Rose
☐ Trans. Magenta

☐ *Geranium Red + Cranberry 3:1

☐ ARC Quinacridone Red Violet

NOTES

BRAND	COLOR	COLOR

T C S # RV-1-2-8

AMERICANA	☐ Napa Red S: Black Plum H: Cherry Red
CERAMCOAT	☐ Mendocino Red S: Sonoma H: Pink Quartz
FOLK ART	☐ Berry Wine S: Licorice H: Ballet Pink
JO SONJA	☐ Trans Magenta (L)
1837 LEGACY	☐ *Geranium Red + Cranberry 1:1
OIL EQUIV.	☐ ARC Permanent Magenta, WN Permanent Alizarin Crimson

NOTES

T C S # RV-1-4-6

| ☐ *Royal Fuchsia + Napa Red 1:1 |
| ☐ Raspberry
S: Black Cherry H: Tangerine |
| ☐ *Alizarin Crimson + Pink 2:1 |
| ☐ *Plum Pink + Rose Pink 3:1 |
| ☐ *Geranium Red + Winter Wine 2:1 |
| ☐ *WN Bright Red + White +
French Ultramarine 4:2:1 |

NOTES

T C S # RV-2-2-8

AMERICANA	☐ Red Violet S: Black Plum H: Fuchsia
CERAMCOAT	☐ Magenta S: Royal Plum H: Lilac Dusk
FOLK ART	☐ Fuchsia S: Raspberry Wine H: Baby Pink
JO SONJA	☐ *Trans. Magenta + Burgundy 2:1
1837 LEGACY	☐ *Geranium Red + Velvet Plum 4:1
OIL EQUIV.	☐ *WN Magenta + Alizarin Crimson + White 2:1:1

NOTES

T C S # RV-2-4-2

| ☐ Petal Pink
S: Royal Fuchsia H: Pink Chiffon |
| ☐ *White + Royal Fuchsia 2:1 |
| ☐ *White + Light Fuchsia 1:1 |
| ☐ *White + Brilliant Magenta + Brilliant Green 3:2:T |
| ☐ *White + Geranium Red 1:1 |
| ☐ *GRUM White + Thalo Red Rose +
Ultramarine. Blue 8:4:1 |

NOTES

T C S # RV-2-4-3

AMERICANA	☐ *Royal Fuchsia + White 1:1
CERAMCOAT	☐ *White + Royal Fuchsia 2:1
FOLK ART	☐ Light Fuchsia S: Fuchsia H: Ballet Pink
JO SONJA	☐ *Brilliant Magenta + Opal 1:1
1837 LEGACY	☐ *Pink Begonia + White 2:1
OIL EQUIV.	☐ *GRUM White + Thalo Red Rose + Ultramarine Blue 6:6:1

NOTES

T C S # RV-2-4-7

| ☐ *Royal Fuchsia + Plum 8:1 |
| ☐ Royal Fuchsia
S: Mulberry H: Pink Quartz |
| ☐ *Fuchsia + Hot Pink 8:1 |
| ☐ Brilliant Magenta |
| ☐ *Geranium Red + Pink Begonia 1:1 |
| ☐ ARC Brilliant Magenta
WN Permanent Magenta |

NOTES

BRAND	COLOR	COLOR

T C S # RV-2-4-8

AMERICANA	☐ *Napa Red + Royal Fuchsia + Dioxazine Purple 2:1:1
CERAMCOAT	☐ Mulberry S: Black H: Royal Fuchsia
FOLK ART	☐ *Berry Wine + Purple Passion 4:1
JO SONJA	☐ *Trans Magenta + Plum Pink 1:1
1837 LEGACY	☐ *Velvet Plum + Cranberry 1:1
OIL EQUIV.	☐ WN Magenta

NOTES

T C S # RV-3-2-4

AMERICANA	☐ *Orchid + Royal Fuchsia 5:1
CERAMCOAT	☐ Lilac Dusk S: Grape H: Lilac Dusk + White 1:1
FOLK ART	☐ *Orchid + Fuchsia 4:1
JO SONJA	☐ *Opal + Amethyst + Trans. Magenta 1:1:1
1837 LEGACY	☐ Pink Begonia S: Velvet Plum H: Wild Rose
OIL EQUIV.	☐ *WN Cobalt Violet + White + Alizarin Crimson 6:2:1

NOTES

T C S # RV-3-2-7

AMERICANA	☐ *Dioxazine Purple + True Red 2:1
CERAMCOAT	☐ Grape S: Vintage Wine H: Lilac Dust
FOLK ART	☐ *Plum Pudding + Raspberry Wine 3:1
JO SONJA	☐ *Trans. Magenta + Dioxazine Purple (T)
1837 LEGACY	☐ Velvet Plum S: Plum H: Pink Begonia
OIL EQUIV.	☐ *WN Purple Lake + Alizarin Crimson 3:1

NOTES

T C S # RV-3-2-8

AMERICANA	☐ *Plum + Black Plum 3:1
CERAMCOAT	☐ *Grape + Black 8:1
FOLK ART	☐ Pure Magenta (AP) S: Pure Black H: Light Fuchsia
JO SONJA	☐ *Red Violet + Purple Madder 4:1
1837 LEGACY	☐ *Velvet Plum + Plum 3:1
OIL EQUIV.	☐ WN Purple Madder Alizarin

NOTES

T C S # RV-5-2-3

AMERICANA	☐ Orchid S: Pansy Lavender H: Orchid + White 1:1
CERAMCOAT	☐ *Lilac + Lilac Dust 1:1
FOLK ART	☐ Orchid S: Red Violet H: White
JO SONJA	☐ *White + Amethyst 2:1
1837 LEGACY	☐ *Pink Begonia + White 1:1
OIL EQUIV.	☐ *WN White + Magenta 4:1

NOTES

T C S # RV-5-2-7

AMERICANA	☐ *Dioxazine Purple + True Red 2:1
CERAMCOAT	☐ Egg Plant S: Black H: Lilac Dust
FOLK ART	☐ Red Violet S: Licorice H: Heather
JO SONJA	☐ *Trans. Magenta + Dioxazine Purple 4:1
1837 LEGACY	☐ *Velvet Plum + Purple 1:1
OIL EQUIV.	☐ WN Cobalt Violet

NOTES

T C S # RV-5-8-2

AMERICANA	☐ Taupe S: Mauve H: Taupe + White 1:1
CERAMCOAT	☐ Taupe S: Napa H: Taupe + White 1:1
FOLK ART	☐ *Milkshake + Plum Pudding 10:1
JO SONJA	☐ *Opal + Amethyst 9:1
1837 LEGACY	☐ Lilac Grey S: Purple Sage H: Soft Lilac
OIL EQUIV.	☐ *WN White + Ivory Black + Bt. Umber + REM Alizarin Crimson 14:4:1:1

NOTES

T C S # RV-5-8-4

AMERICANA	☐ *Mauve + Taupe 2:1
CERAMCOAT	☐ Dusty Plum S: Dusty Purple H: Taupe
FOLK ART	☐ *Tapioca + Plum Pudding 3:1
JO SONJA	☐ *Opal + Amethyst 6:1
1837 LEGACY	☐ Purple Sage S: Plum Wine H: Soft Lilac
OIL EQUIV.	☐ *WN French Ultramarine + Aliz. Crimson + White + Raw Sienna 3:3:2:1

NOTES

T C S # RV-5-8-5

AMERICANA	☐ *Lavender + Cranberry Wine 3:1
CERAMCOAT	☐ Wisteria S: Napa H: Lilac Dust
FOLK ART	☐ *Plum Chiffon + White 2:1
JO SONJA	☐ *Amethyst + Indian Red Oxide + White 2:1:1
1837 LEGACY	☐ Pansey Purple S: Mulberry H: Amethyst
OIL EQUIV.	☐ *WN French Ultramarine + Alizarin Crimson + White 2:2:1

NOTES

T C S # RV-5-8-8

AMERICANA	☐ *Cranberry Wine + Dioxazine Purple 3:1
CERAMCOAT	☐ Dusty Purple S: Payne's Grey H: Dusty Plum
FOLK ART	☐ Purple Passion S: Licorice H: Orchid
JO SONJA	☐ *Amethyst + Indian Red Oxide 2:1
1837 LEGACY	☐ Mulberry S: Black H: Pink Begonia
OIL EQUIV.	☐ *WN Alizarin Crimson + French Ultramarine + White 3:3:1

NOTES

T C S # RV-5-8-9

AMERICANA	☐ Plum S: Black Plum H: Fuchsia
CERAMCOAT	☐ Royal Plum S: Black H: Magenta
FOLK ART	☐ Plum Pudding S: Licorice H: Heather
JO SONJA	☐ *Indian Red Oxide + Amethyst 1:1
1837 LEGACY	☐ Mulberry (L) S: Black H: Pink Begonia
OIL EQUIV.	☐ WN Permanent Mauve

NOTES

T C S # RV-5-9-8

AMERICANA	☐ *Cranberry Wine + Dioxazine Purple 1:1
CERAMCOAT	☐ Napa Wine S: Vintage Wine H: Dusty Plum
FOLK ART	☐ Plum Chiffon S: Licorice H: Orchid
JO SONJA	☐ *Amethyst + Indian Red Oxide 1:1
1837 LEGACY	☐ Plum Wine S: Mulberry H: Purple Sage
OIL EQUIV.	☐ *WN White + Alizarin Crimson + French Ultramarine + Burnt Umber 4:2:2:1

NOTES

BRAND	COLOR	COLOR

TCS #RV-6-9-7

AMERICANA	☐ *Neutral Grey + Pansy Lavender 3:1
CERAMCOAT	☐ *Hippo Grey + Napa 2:1
FOLK ART	☐ *Dapple Gray + Violet Pansy 3:1
JO SONJA	☐ *Amethyst + Raw Umber 1:1 Jo Sonja Bkg Lavender
1837 LEGACY	☐ *Silver Fox + Plum Wine 1:1
OIL EQUIV.	☐ *PERM Ivory Black + REM Bt. Carmine + WN White + Raw Sienna 6:2:2:1

NOTES

TCS #RV-9-2-3

	☐ *Orchid + Lavender 4:1
	☐ Lilac S: Wisteria H: Ice Storm
	☐ *Heather + Sweetheart Pink 1:1
	☐ Amethyst
	☐ Amethyst S: Purple H: Soft Lilac
	☐ *WN White + Cobalt Violet 2:1

NOTES

TCS #RV-9-2-5

AMERICANA	☐ *Lavender + Orchid 1:1
CERAMCOAT	☐ *Vintage Wine + White 1:1
FOLK ART	☐ Heather S: Purple Passion H: Orchid
JO SONJA	☐ *Amethyst + Dioxazine Purple 8:1
1837 LEGACY	☐ *Amethyst + Purple 1:1
OIL EQUIV.	☐ *WN Alizarin Crimson + French Ultramarine + White 3:4:8

NOTES

TCS #RV-9-2-8

	☐ Pansy Lavender S: Royal Purple H: Orchid
	☐ Vintage Wine S: Black H: Lilac
	☐ *Red Violet + Dioxazine Purple 3:1
	☐ *Amethyst + Dioxazine Purple 3:2
	☐ Plum (D) S: Black H: Amethyst
	☐ WN Cobalt Violet Dark

NOTES

TCS #RV-9-2-9

AMERICANA	☐ Royal Purple S: Dioxazine Purple H: Pansy Lavender
CERAMCOAT	☐ Vintage Wine (L) S: Black H: Lilac
FOLK ART	☐ *Dioxazine Purple + Heather 2:1
JO SONJA	☐ *Amethyst + Dioxazine Purple 1:1
1837 LEGACY	☐ Plum S: Black H: Amethyst
OIL EQUIV.	☐ PRI Cobalt Violet Hue, *WN Alizarin Crimson + French Ultramarine 1:1

NOTES

TCS #RV-9-6-1

	☐ *Grey Sky + Orchid 2:1
	☐ Ice Storm Violet S: Lavender H: White
	☐ *Gray Mist + Orchid 10:1
	☐ *Warm White + Amethyst 12:1
	☐ Soft Lilac S: Iris H: White
	☐ *WN White + French Ultramarine + Alizarin Crimson 10:2:1

NOTES

BRAND	COLOR	COLOR

TCS #RV-9-6-5

AMERICANA	☐ Summer Lilac S: Pansy Lavender H: Lilac
CERAMCOAT	☐ *Lilac + Lavender 3:1
FOLK ART	☐ *Purple Lilac + Orchid 4:1
JO SONJA	☐ *White + Amethyst + French Blue 3:2:T
1837 LEGACY	☐ *Iris + Lilac Grey 2:1
OIL EQUIV.	☐ *WN White + French Ultramarine + Alizarin Crimson 4:2:2

NOTES

TCS # VI-4-1-7

	☐ *Dioxazine Purple + Cadmium Red (T)
	☐ *Purple + Napthol Red Light (T)
	☐ Violet Pansy S: Licorice H: Purple Lilac
	☐ *Diox. Purple + White + Nap. Crimson 1:1:T
	☐ *Purple + Napthol Red Light (T)
	☐ *WN White + Mauve + Perm. Rose + Burnt Umber + Ultramar. Blue 12:2:2:1:1

NOTES

TCS # VI-5-1-2

AMERICANA	☐ Lilac S: Orchid H: Lilac + White 1:1
CERAMCOAT	☐ *White + Lilac 6:1
FOLK ART	☐ *White + Heather 6:1
JO SONJA	☐ *White + Dioxazine Purple 12:1
1837 LEGACY	☐ *White + Amethyst 6:1
OIL EQUIV.	☐ *WN White + Cobalt Violet 3:1

NOTES

TCS # VI-5-1-4

	☐ *Lavender + White 2:1
	☐ G.P. Purple S: Purple H: Ice Storm Violet
	☐ Lavender (D) S: Red Violet H: Lavender Sachet
	☐ *Amethyst + Prussian Blue (T)
	☐ Iris S: Purple H: Soft Lilac
	☐ *WN White + Dioxazine Purple 2:1

NOTES

TCS #VI-5-1-5

AMERICANA	☐ Lavender S: Dioxazine Purple H: Lavender + White 1:1
CERAMCOAT	☐ *Purple + White 2:1
FOLK ART	☐ Lavender S: Red Violet H: Lavender Sachet
JO SONJA	☐ *Diox. Purple + White 1:1
1837 LEGACY	☐ Lavender S: Purple H: Soft Lilac
OIL EQUIV.	☐ *WN Permanent Rose + Winsor Blue + White 4:2:2

NOTES

TCS #VI-5-1-7

	☐ Dioxazine Purple S: Payne's Grey H: Lavender
	☐ Purple S: Vintage Wine H: G.P. Purple
	☐ Purple S: Licorice H: Lavender
	☐ Dioxazine Purple (D)
	☐ Purple S: Plum H: Soft Lilac
	☐ WN Winsor Violet (Dioxazine)

NOTES

BRAND **COLOR** **COLOR**

T C S # VI-5-1-9

AMERICANA	☐ *Dioxazine Purple + Prussian Blue (T)
CERAMCOAT	☐ *Purple + Midnight (T)
FOLK ART	☐ Dioxazine Purple (AP) S: Pure Black H: Lavender
JO SONJA	☐ Dioxazine Purple
1837 LEGACY	☐ *Purple + Velvet Night 6:1
OIL EQUIV.	☐ ARC Dioxazine Violet, WN Mauve (Blue Shade)

NOTES

T C S # VI-5-3-7

| ☐ *Dioxazine Purple + Lavender 2:1 |
| ☐ *Purple + G.P. Purple 2:1 |
| ☐ *Purple + Lavender 2:1 |
| ☐ Brilliant Violet |
| ☐ *Lavender + Purple 1:1 |
| ☐ WN Ultramarine Violet |

NOTES

T C S # VI-5-8-5

AMERICANA	☐ *Lavender + Neutral Gray 3:1
CERAMCOAT	☐ Lavender S: Vintage Wine H: Ice Storm Violet
FOLK ART	☐ Purple Lilac S: Violet Pansy H: Lavender Sachet
JO SONJA	☐ *Amethyst + Nimbus Grey 4:1
1837 LEGACY	☐ *Lavender + Lilac Grey 4:1
OIL EQUIV.	☐ *WN White + Mauve + French Ultramarine + Cadmium Yellow Pale 20:4:1:1

NOTES

T C S # VI-5-9-4

| ☐ *Pansy Lavender + Ice Blue 1:1 |
| ☐ *Lavender + Cadet Grey 1:1 |
| ☐ Gray Plum
S: Dark Plum H: Lavender Sachet |
| ☐ *Nimbus Grey + Brilliant Violet + White 1:1:1 |
| ☐ *Iris + Silver Fox 1:1 |
| ☐ *WN White + Ivory Black +
REM Burnt Carmine 6:3:1 |

NOTES

T C S #VI-5-9-7

AMERICANA	☐ *Royal Purple + Neutral Grey 1:1
CERAMCOAT	☐ *Lavender + Hippo Grey 2:1
FOLK ART	☐ Dark Plum S: Payne's Gray H: Gray Plum
JO SONJA	☐ *Brilliant Violet + Black 3:1
1837 LEGACY	☐ *Lavender + Pioneer Grey 1:1
OIL EQUIV.	☐ *REM Black + Bt. Carmine + Indigo + White 4:1:1:2

NOTES

T C S #VI-9-6-6

| ☐ Violet Haze
S: Dioxazine Purple H: Lilac |
| ☐ *Purple Dusk + Hammered Iron 6:1 |
| ☐ *Periwinkle + Slate Blue 3:1 |
| ☐ *White + French Blue + Diox. Purple 2:1:1 |
| ☐ *Dover Blue + Pink Begonia 1:1 |
| ☐ *WN French Ultramarine + White +
Alizarin Crimson 4:2:1 |

NOTES

COLOR   COLOR

TCS # BV-2-6-1

AMERICANA   □ *Grey Sky + Lilac 2:1

CERAMCOAT   □ *White + Lavender 8:1

FOLK ART   □ Lavender Sachet
              S: Periwinkle H: White

JO SONJA   □ *Warm White + Dioxazine Purple 12:1

1837 LEGACY   □ *Soft Lilac + Shy Violet 8:1

OIL EQUIV.   □ *WN White + Prussian Blue +
              Alizarin Crimson 40:1:2

NOTES

TCS # BV-5-2-4

AMERICANA   □ *Country Blue + Lavender 4:1

CERAMCOAT   □ Bahama Purple
              S: Purple Dusk H: White
              □ *Light Periwinkle + Lavender 4:1

JO SONJA   □ *White + Diox. Purple + Storm Blue 6:1:1

1837 LEGACY   □ *Iris + Heavenly Blue 1:1

OIL EQUIV.   □ *WN French Ultramarine + White +
              Alizarin Crimson 4:2:1

NOTES

TCS #BV-5-2-6

AMERICANA   □ *Blue Violet + Dioxazine Purple 3:1

CERAMCOAT   □ Rhythm 'N Blue
              S: Purple H: Bahama Purple

FOLK ART   □ *Brilliant Blue + Night Sky 4:1

JO SONJA   □ *Pacific Blue + Brilliant Violet 1:1

1837 LEGACY   □ *Purple + Thalo Blue 3:1

OIL EQUIV.   □ *WN French Ultramarine + Winsor Violet +
              White 4:2:1

NOTES

TCS # BV-5-2-8

AMERICANA   □ *Dioxazine Purple + Ultra Blue Deep 1:1

CERAMCOAT   □ *Purple + Navy Blue 1:1

FOLK ART   □ Night Sky
              S: Licorice H: Light Periwinkle
              □ *Dioxazine Purple + Ultra Blue Deep 1:1

1837 LEGACY   □ *Purple + Blazer Blue 5:1

OIL EQUIV.   □ *WN French Ultramarine +Alizarin Crimson 5:1

NOTES

TCS #BV-5-3-3

AMERICANA   □ Wisteria
              S: Deep Periwinkle H: White

CERAMCOAT   □ *Bahama Purple + Hydrangea Pink +
              White 2:1:1

FOLK ART   □ *White + Periwinkle 3:1

JO SONJA   □ *White + Pacific Blue + Brilliant Magenta +
              Turners Yellow 10:2:1:T

1837 LEGACY   □ *Iris + Forget-Me-Not Blue + White +
              Canola 2:2:1:T

OIL EQUIV.   □ *WN White + GRUM Thalo Red Rose +
              WN Ultramarine Blue 20:2:1

NOTES

TCS # BV-5-3-6

AMERICANA   □ Deep Periwinkle
              S: Admiral Blue H: Wisteria

CERAMCOAT   □ *Bahama Purple + Purple Dusk 1:1

FOLK ART   □ *Periwinkle + White 2:1

JO SONJA   □ *Pacific Blue + Brilliant Magenta + White +
              Turners Yellow 3:1:1:T

1837 LEGACY   □ *Electric Blue + Purple 1:1

OIL EQUIV.   □ *WN White + Winsor Blue +
              GRUM Thalo Red Rose 8:1:1

NOTES

BRAND	COLOR	COLOR

T C S # BV-5-4-6

AMERICANA	☐ *Country Blue + Dioxazine Purple 3:1
CERAMCOAT	☐ Purple Dusk S: Payne's Grey H: Bahama Purple
FOLK ART	☐ *Periwinkle + Purple Lilac 2:1
JO SONJA	☐ *Warm White + Diox. Purple + Storm Blue 2:2:1 Jo Sonja Bkg Azure
1837 LEGACY	☐ *Lavender + Phantom Blue 4:1
OIL EQUIV.	☐ *WN French Ultramarine + Alizarin Crimson + White 4:2:1

NOTES

T C S # BV-5-4-8

AMERICANA	☐ *Uniform Blue + Orchid 1:1
CERAMCOAT	☐ *Liberty Blue + Purple 1:1
FOLK ART	☐ Periwinkle S: Blue Ink H: Light Periwinkle
JO SONJA	☐ *Amethyst + Prussian Blue 4:1
1837 LEGACY	☐ *Purple + Ontario Blue 1:1
OIL EQUIV.	☐ *WN Prussian Blue + Alizarin Crimson + White 1:2:5

NOTES

T C S # BV-6-8-3

AMERICANA	☐ *French Gray/Blue + Ice Blue 1:1
CERAMCOAT	☐ *Dolphin + Ice Storm 2:1
FOLK ART	☐ Whipped Berry S: Slate Blue H: Icy White
JO SONJA	☐ *Warm White + Sapphire + Amethyst 8:2:1
1837 LEGACY	☐ *Oxford Grey + Soft Lilac 2:1
OIL EQUIV.	☐ *WN French Ultramarine + Burnt Umber +White 3:1:12

NOTES

T C S # BV-7-8-3

AMERICANA	☐ *Flesh + Country Blue 3:1
CERAMCOAT	☐ Lavender Lace S: Heritage Blue H: Ice Storm Violet
FOLK ART	☐ *Cotton Candy + Porcelain Blue 1:1
JO SONJA	☐ *Warm White + Sapphire + Dioxazine Purple 8:2:1
1837 LEGACY	☐ Shy Violet S: Purple H: White
OIL EQUIV.	☐ *WN White + REM Indigo Extra + GRUM Thalo Red Rose 25:3:1

NOTES

T C S # BV-8-3-3

AMERICANA	☐ *Country Blue + White 2:1
CERAMCOAT	☐ *Periwinkle + White 2:1
FOLK ART	☐ Baby Blue S: French Blue H: White
JO SONJA	☐ *White + Storm Blue 15:1
1837 LEGACY	☐ *Shy Violet + Wedgewood Blue 2:1
OIL EQUIV.	☐ *WN White + French Ultramarine + Burnt Umber + Prussian Blue 60:7:1:1

NOTES

T C S # BV-8-3-4

AMERICANA	☐ Country Blue S: Sapphire H: Country Blue + White 1:1
CERAMCOAT	☐ Periwinkle Blue S: Navy Blue H: Chambray Blue
FOLK ART	☐ Light Periwinkle S: Blue Ink H: White
JO SONJA	☐ *White + Sapphire Blue + Amethyst 2:2:1
1837 LEGACY	☐ Forget-Me-Not Blue S: Phantom Blue H: Snowball
OIL EQUIV.	☐ *WN White + French Ultramarine + Burnt Umber 15:7:1

NOTES

	T C S # BV-8-3-6
AMERICANA	☐ *Blue Violet + White 1:1
CERAMCOAT	☐ Blue Lagoon S: Opaque Blue H: Blue Heaven
FOLK ART	☐ *Cobalt + White 2:1
JO SONJA	☐ Pacific Blue
1837 LEGACY	☐ *Electric Blue + Shy Violet 2:1
OIL EQUIV.	☐ *WN White + GRUM Ultra. Blue + REM Alizarin Crimson 10:8:1

NOTES

	T C S # BV-9-1-8
	☐ Blue Violet S: Payne's Grey H: Blue Violet + White 1:1
	☐ Ultra Blue S: Navy Blue H: Blue Mist
	☐ *Cobalt + Dioxazine Purple 12:1
	☐ *Ultra Blue Deep + Dioxazine Purple 12:1
	☐ Electric Blue S: Thalo Blue H: Blue Birds
	☐ *WN French Ultramarine Blue + White 3:1

NOTES

	T C S # BV-9-6-7
AMERICANA	☐ *Blue Violet + Prussian Blue 5:1
CERAMCOAT	☐ *Copen Blue + Purple 4:1
FOLK ART	☐ Sterling Blue S: Blue Ink H: Baby Blue
JO SONJA	☐ *Sapphire + Dioxazine Purple 6:1
1837 LEGACY	☐ *Sapphire Blue + Phantom Blue 2:1
OIL EQUIV.	☐ *WN White + French Ultramarine + Burnt Umber + Alizarin Crimson + 10:10:2:1

NOTES

	T C S # BV-9-6-8
	☐ Admiral Blue S: Payne's Grey H: Country Blue
	☐ *Prussian Blue + Purple 1:1
	☐ Midnight S: Licorice H: White
	☐ *Storm Blue + Dioxazine Purple 1:1
	☐ *Purple + Prussian Blue 2:1
	☐ *WN French Ultramarine + Burnt Umber + Alizarin Crimson 4:1:1

NOTES

	T C S # BV-9-6-9
AMERICANA	☐ *Navy + Dioxazine Purple 3:1
CERAMCOAT	☐ *Midnight Blue + Periwinkle Blue 2:1
FOLK ART	☐ Blue Ink S: Licorice H: Periwinkle
JO SONJA	☐ *Pthalo Blue + Dioxazine Purple 5:1
1837 LEGACY	☐ *Velvet Night + Purple 1:1
OIL EQUIV.	☐ ARC Royal Blue

NOTES

	T C S # BV-9-7-8
	☐ *Blue Violet + Violet Haze 3:1
	☐ Purple Smoke S: Dark Night Blue H: Purple Dusk
	☐ *Midnight + Lavender 3:1
	☐ *Pacific Blue + Dioxazine Purple 4:1
	☐ *Phantom Blue + Purple 2:1
	☐ *WN French Ultramarine + Alizarin Crimson + Payne's Gray + White 2:2:1:1

NOTES

BLUE 3-3-2 / BLUE 4-5-6

T C S # BL-3-3-2

AMERICANA	☐ *White + Country Blue 6:1
CERAMCOAT	☐ Violet Ice S: Periwinkle Blue H: White
FOLK ART	☐ *White + Porcelain Blue 6:1
JO SONJA	☐ *White + Ultra Blue Deep 8:1
1837 LEGACY	☐ *Snowball + Shy Violet 6:1
OIL EQUIV.	☐ *WN White + French Ultramarine + Winsor Violet 12:1:1

NOTES

ì ı / BL-3-3-5

AMERICANA	☐ *Sapphire + White 1:1
CERAMCOAT	☐ *Liberty Blue + White 1:1
FOLK ART	☐ French Blue S: Midnight H: Icy White ☐ *Sapphire + White 1:1
1837 LEGACY	☐ *Ontario Blue + White 1:1
OIL EQUIV.	☐ *WN White + French Ultramarine + Burnt Umber + Prussian Blue 22:7:1:1

NOTES

T C S # BL-3-8-8

AMERICANA	☐ *Uniform Blue + Charcoal Grey 5:1
CERAMCOAT	☐ Heritage Blue S: Charcoal H: Tide Pool
FOLK ART	☐ *Heartland Blue + Charcoal Grey 4:1
JO SONJA	☐ *French Blue + Plum Pink 4:1
1837 LEGACY	☐ Slate Grey S: Velvet Night H: French Blue Grey
OIL EQUIV.	☐ ARC Violet Grey

NOTES

T C S # BL-4-2-6

AMERICANA	☐ Sapphire S: True Blue H: Sapphire + White 1:1
CERAMCOAT	☐ *Ultra Blue + Pthalo Blue 3:1
FOLK ART	☐ *True Blue + Light Blue 4:1
JO SONJA	☐ *Ultra Blue Deep + Nimbus Grey 3:1
1837 LEGACY	☐ *Blazer Blue + Blue Birds 2:1
OIL EQUIV.	☐ *WN Cobalt Blue + Ivory Black + White 4:1:1

NOTES

T C S # BL-4-5-5

AMERICANA	☐ *Sapphire + Blue Violet 4:1
CERAMCOAT	☐ Denim Blue S: Navy Blue H: Blue Mist
FOLK ART	☐ *True Blue + French Blue 4:1
JO SONJA	☐ *Sapphire + Ultra Blue 1:1
1837 LEGACY	☐ *Aegean Blue + Purple 3:1
OIL EQUIV.	☐ *SHIV Cerulean Blue + WN White + Ultra. Blue 4:1:1

NOTES

T C S # BL-4-5-6

AMERICANA	☐ *Sapphire + Williamsburg Blue 4:1
CERAMCOAT	☐ Liberty Blue S: Nightfall Blue H: Lavender Lace
FOLK ART	☐ *True Blue + French blue 2:1
JO SONJA	☐ Sapphire
1837 LEGACY	☐ Ontario Blue S: Prussian Blue H: Heavenly Blue
OIL EQUIV.	☐ *WN French Ultramarine + Prussian Blue + Burnt Umber + White 5:1:2:5

NOTES

T C S # BL-4-8-4

AMERICANA	☐ Light French Blue S: French Grey/Blue H: Ice Blue
CERAMCOAT	☐ Dolphin Grey S: Adriatic Blue H: Lavender Lace
FOLK ART	☐ Amish Blue (D) S: Denim Blue H: Lavender Sachet
JO SONJA	☐ *White + French Blue 3:1
1837 LEGACY	☐ Oxford Grey S: French Blue Grey H: White
OIL EQUIV.	☐ *WN White + REM Warm Grey + Indigo Extra 3:2:1

NOTES

T C S # BL-4-8-5

AMERICANA	☐ *White + French Grey/Blue 2:1
CERAMCOAT	☐ Dolphin Grey (L) S: Adriatic Blue H: Lavender Lace
FOLK ART	☐ Amish Blue S: Denim Blue H: Lavender Sachet
JO SONJA	☐ *White + French Blue 2:1
1837 LEGACY	☐ French Blue Grey S: Slate Grey H: Oxford Grey
OIL EQUIV.	☐ *WN French Ultramarine + Burnt Umber + White 3:1:8

NOTES

T C S # BL-4-8-8

AMERICANA	☐ *Uniform Blue + Charcoal Grey 3:1
CERAMCOAT	☐ Adriatic Blue S: Black H: Dolphin Grey
FOLK ART	☐ Slate Blue S: Indigo H: Lavender Sachet
JO SONJA	☐ *French Blue + Sapphire 2:1
1837 LEGACY	☐ Superior Blue S: Velvet Night H: Oxford Grey
OIL EQUIV.	☐ *WN French Ultramarine + Burnt Umber + White 3:1:3

NOTES

T C S # BL-4-9-2

AMERICANA	☐ Ice Blue S: Blue/Grey Mist H: Ice Blue + White 1:1
CERAMCOAT	☐ *Blue Wisp + Drizzle Grey 1:1
FOLK ART	☐ Ice Blue (AP) S: Amish Blue H: Icy White
JO SONJA	☐ *Warm White + Payne's Grey 12:1
1837 LEGACY	☐ *Atlantic Surf + Pelican 1:1
OIL EQUIV.	☐ *WN White + French Ultramarine + Burnt Umber + Cadmium Yellow Pale 15:2:1:1

NOTES

T C S # BL-4-9-5

AMERICANA	☐ Blue/Grey Mist S: Payne's Grey H: Ice Blue
CERAMCOAT	☐ *Bridgeport + Adriatic (T)
FOLK ART	☐ Blue Gray Dust (Disc.) or *Amish Blue + Medium Gray 4:1
JO SONJA	☐ *Nimbus Gray + Storm Blue (T) + Gold Ox.(T)
1837 LEGACY	☐ Pioneer Grey S: Rhino Grey H: Dove Grey
OIL EQUIV.	☐ *WN White + GRUM Greenish Umber + WN Bt. Umber + Ultra. Blue 8:4:1:1

NOTES

T C S # BL-4-9-8

AMERICANA	☐ *French Grey/Blue + Black 4:1
CERAMCOAT	☐ Fjord Blue S: Payne's Grey H: Tide Pool
FOLK ART	☐ *Amish Blue + Charcoal 4:1
JO SONJA	☐ *French Blue + Black 4:1 Jo Sonja Bkg Dolphin Blue
1837 LEGACY	☐ Smoky Blue S: Black H: Dover Blue
OIL EQUIV.	☐ *REM Payne's Gray + White + Indigo Extra + WN Burnt Umber 8:4:1:1

NOTES

	COLOR	COLOR

TCS #BL-4-9-9

AMERICANA	☐ *Prussian Blue + Black (T)
CERAMCOAT	☐ Dark Night Blue S: Black H: Dolphin Gray
FOLK ART	☐ Payne's Gray (AP) S: Pure Black H: Amish Blue
JO SONJA	☐ Storm Blue Jo Sonja Bkg Galaxy Blue
1837 LEGACY	☐ Kohl Blue S: Black H: Phantom Blue
OIL EQUIV.	☐ REM Indigo, WN Payne's Gray

NOTES

ì ı / BL-5-1-1

☐ *White + Dove Grey 10:1
☐ *White + Drizzle Grey 12:1
☐ Winter White S: Baby Blue H: None
☐ *White + Nimbus Grey (T)
☐ *White + Pelican 20:1
☐ *WN White + French Ultramarine + Burnt Umber 50:2:1

NOTES

TCS # BL-5-1-5

AMERICANA	☐ Primary Blue S: Deep Midnight H: Baby Blue
CERAMCOAT	☐ Phthalo Blue S: Midnight H: Blue Jay
FOLK ART	☐ True Blue S: Midnight H: French Blue
JO SONJA	☐ Ultramarine Blue
1837 LEGACY	☐ Thalo Blue S: Kohl Blue H: Blue Birds
OIL EQUIV.	☐ ARC Sky Blue, WN Blue Red Shade

NOTES

TCS # BL-5-1-6

☐ True Blue S: Prussian Blue H: True Blue + White 1:1
☐ *Ultra Blue + Navy 1:1
☐ Brilliant Ultramarine (AP) S: Blue Ink H: Light Blue
☐ Ultramarine Blue Deep
☐ *Electric Blue + Blazer Blue 1:1
☐ ARC Ultramarine Blue, WN French Ultramarine

NOTES

TCS #BL-5-1-9

AMERICANA	☐ *Prussian Blue + Ultra Blue Deep 2:1
CERAMCOAT	☐ Blue Velvet S: None H: Copen Blue
FOLK ART	☐ Navy Blue S: Licorice H: Settler's Blue
JO SONJA	☐ *Storm Blue + Ultra Blue 2:1
1837 LEGACY	☐ *Velvet Night + Thalo Blue 2:1
OIL EQUIV.	☐ WN Indanthrene Blue

NOTES

TCS #BL-5-2-2

☐ Baby Blue S: Sapphire H: Baby Blue + White 1:1
☐ Blue Heaven S: Copen Blue H: Blue Mist
☐ Light Blue S: Heartland Blue H: Blue Ribbon
☐ *White + Sapphire 6:1
☐ Heavenly Blue S: Blue Birds H: Snowball
☐ *WN Winsor Blue + French Ultramarine + White 1:2:30

NOTES

T C S # BL-5-2-4

AMERICANA   ☐ *True Blue + White 1:1

CERAMCOAT   ☐ Blue Jay
       S: Manganese Blue H: Blue Mist

FOLK ART   ☐ *Blue Ribbon + White 1:1

JO SONJA   ☐ *White + Pthalo Blue 3:1

1837 LEGACY   ☐ Blue Birds
       S: Sapphire Blue H: Gentle Blue

OIL EQUIV.   ☐ *WN French Ultramarine + Cerulean Blue +
       White 3:2:1

NOTES

T C S # BL-5-2-5

☐ Ultra Blue Deep (D)
   S: Payne's Grey H: Sapphire
☐ Opaque Blue
   S: Payne's Grey H: Blue Jay
☐ Brilliant Blue
   S: Midnight H: Light Periwinkle
☐ *Pthalo Blue + Ultramarine Blue 1:1

☐ *Electric Blue + Thalo Blue 3:1

☐ ARC Cobalt Blue Hue,
   PRI Cobalt Blue Hue

NOTES

T C S # BL-5-2-6

AMERICANA   ☐ Ultra Blue Deep
       S: Payne's Grey H: Sapphire

CERAMCOAT   ☐ Navy Blue
       S: Payne's Grey H: Blue Jay

FOLK ART   ☐ *Cobalt + Midnight 3:1

JO SONJA   ☐ Pthalo Blue

1837 LEGACY   ☐ Blazer Blue
       S: Velvet Night H: Sapphire Blue

OIL EQUIV.   ☐ ARC Pthalo Blue,
       PRI Ultramarine Blue

NOTES

T C S # BL-5-2-7

☐ Prussian Blue
   S: Payne's Grey H: Sapphire
☐ *Navy Blue + Midnight 4:1

☐ Prussian Blue (AP)
   S: Pure Black H: Cobalt
☐ Prussian Blue Hue

☐ *Blazer Blue + Velvet Night 2:1

☐ ARC Prussian Blue,
   *WN Ultramarine Blue + Burnt Umber +
   Prussian Blue 2:1:1

NOTES

T C S # BL-5-2-8

AMERICANA   ☐ Deep Midnight Blue
       S: Payne's Grey H: Uniform Blue

CERAMCOAT   ☐ Midnight Blue
       S: Black H: Bonnie Blue

FOLK ART   ☐ Indigo
       S: Licorice H: French Blue

JO SONJA   ☐ *Payne's Grey + Storm Blue + Sapphire 2:1:1

1837 LEGACY   ☐ Velvet Night
       S: Black H: Sapphire Blue

OIL EQUIV.   ☐ *REM Indigo + White 10:1

NOTES

T C S # BL-5-2-9

☐ Payne's Grey
   S: Lamp (Ebony) Black H: Uniform Blue
☐ Payne's Grey
   S: Black H: Dolphin Grey
☐ *Payne's Gray + Prussian Blue (T)

☐ Payne's Grey

☐ *Velvet Night + Black 4:1

☐ ARC Payne's Grey, GRUM Payne's Gray,
   REM Payne's Gray, WN Indigo

NOTES

BRAND **COLOR** **COLOR**

TCS #BL-5-5-3

AMERICANA	☐ Winter Blue S: Sapphire H: Blue Chiffon
CERAMCOAT	☐ Wedgewood Blue S: Manganese Blue H: Blue Mist
FOLK ART	☐ *Bluebell + White 1:1
JO SONJA	☐ *Smoked Pearl + Sapphire (T)
1837 LEGACY	☐ Wedgewood Blue S: Aegean Blue H: Snowball
OIL EQUIV.	☐ *WN White + REM Indigo Extra + REM Warm Grey 4:2:1

NOTES

ì ı / BL-5-5-5

AMERICANA	☐ *Williamsburg Blue + White (T)
CERAMCOAT	☐ Bonnie Blue S: Midnight Blue H: Blue Mist
FOLK ART	☐ Bluebell S: Bluebonnet H: Icy White
JO SONJA	☐ *Nimbus Grey + Sapphire 2:1
1837 LEGACY	☐ Aegean Blue S: Superior Blue H: Wedgewood Blue
OIL EQUIV.	☐ *WN Prussian Blue + French Ultramarine + Burnt Umber + White 1:2:2:20

NOTES

TCS #BL-5-7-2

AMERICANA	☐ *White + French Grey/Blue 5:1
CERAMCOAT	☐ Chambray Blue S: Tide Pool Blue H: White
FOLK ART	☐ *Porcelain Blue + White 2:1
JO SONJA	☐ *White + French Blue 3:1
1837 LEGACY	☐ *White + Banff Blue 2:1
OIL EQUIV.	☐ *WN White + REM Indigo Extra + REM Warm Grey 6:3:1

NOTES

TCS # BL-5-7-3

AMERICANA	☐ *French Grey/Blue + White 2:1
CERAMCOAT	☐ Tide Pool Blue S: Heritage Blue H: Lavender Lace
FOLK ART	☐ Porcelain Blue S: Denim Blue H: White
JO SONJA	☐ *French Blue + White 2:1 Jo Sonja Bkg Sky Blue
1837 LEGACY	☐ Banff Blue S: Dover Blue H: White
OIL EQUIV.	☐ *WN White + French Ultramarine + Burnt Umber + Alizarin Crimson 20:10:2:1

NOTES

TCS #BL-5-7-4

AMERICANA	☐ French Grey/Blue S: Uniform Blue H: Country Blue
CERAMCOAT	☐ Cape Cod Blue S: Nightfall H: Lavender Lace
FOLK ART	☐ Settler's Blue S: Denim Blue H: Icy White
JO SONJA	☐ *White + French Blue 2:1
1837 LEGACY	☐ Delft Blue S: Dover Blue H: White
OIL EQUIV.	☐ *WN French Ultramarine + Burnt Umber + White 4:1:7

NOTES

TCS #BL-5-7-5

AMERICANA	☐ Williamsburg Blue S: Uniform Blue H: Country Blue
CERAMCOAT	☐ Williamsburg Blue S: Nightfall Blue H: Chambray Blue
FOLK ART	☐ Settler's Blue (L) S: Denim Blue H: Icy White
JO SONJA	☐ *Warm White + Prussian Blue + Ultra Blue + Black 36:2:1:1
1837 LEGACY	☐ Dover Blue S: Phantom Blue H: Wedgewood Blue
OIL EQUIV.	☐ *REM Indigo Extra + WN Terre Verte + White 4:2:1

NOTES

T C S # BL-5-7-7

AMERICANA ☐ Uniform Blue
S: Deep Midnight Blue H: French Grey/Blue

CERAMCOAT ☐ Cadet Blue
S: Blue Velvet H: Tide Pool Blue

FOLK ART ☐ Heartland Blue
S: Licorice H: French Blue

JO SONJA ☐ French Blue (D)

1837 LEGACY ☐ Phantom Blue (D)
S: Velvet Night H: Dover Blue

OIL EQUIV. ☐ *WN French Ultramarine + Burnt Umber + White 3:1:2

NOTES

T C S # BL-5-7-8

☐ Uniform Blue (L)
S: Deep Midnight Blue H: French Grey/Blue
☐ Nightfall Blue
S: Payne's Grey H: Tide Pool
☐ Denim Blue
S: Licorice H: White
☐ French Blue

☐ Phantom Blue
S: Velvet Night H: Dover Blue
☐ *WN White + French Ultramarine + Burnt Umber + Alizarin Crimson 8:5:2:2

NOTES

T C S # BL-5-7-9

AMERICANA ☐ *Uniform Blue + Payne's Grey 3:1

CERAMCOAT ☐ Blue Storm
S: Blue Velvet H: Cape Cod Blue

FOLK ART ☐ *Heartland Blue + Payne's Gray 1:1

JO SONJA ☐ *French Blue + Payne's Grey 1:1

1837 LEGACY ☐ Dark Sapphire Blue
S: Black H: Delft Blue

OIL EQUIV. ☐ *WN Payne's Gray + White 6:1

NOTES

T C S # BL-5-8-7

☐ *Uniform Blue + Light French Blue 1:1

☐ *Williamsburg Blue + Bridgeport 2:1

☐ *Heartland Blue + White 2:1

☐ *Nimbus Grey + French Blue 2:1

☐ Country Slate Blue
S: Smokey Blue H: Delft Blue
☐ *REM White + Indigo + Ivory Black 2:2:1

NOTES

T C S # BL-6-1-1

AMERICANA ☐ *White + Baby Blue 3:1

CERAMCOAT ☐ Glacier Blue
S: Blue Danube H: White

FOLK ART ☐ Icy White
S: Any cool color H: White

JO SONJA ☐ *White + Pthalo Blue 12:1

1837 LEGACY ☐ *Snowball + White 1:1

OIL EQUIV. ☐ *WN Winsor Blue + French Ultramarine + White 1:2:60

NOTES

T C S # BL-6-1-2

☐ Blue Chiffon
S: Winter Blue H: White
☐ Blue Mist
S: Blue Danube H: White
☐ *White + Light Blue 3:1

☐ *White + Pthalo Blue 8:1

☐ Snowball
S: Gentle Blue H: White
☐ *WN White + REM Indigo Extra + WN Terre Verte 12:2:1

NOTES

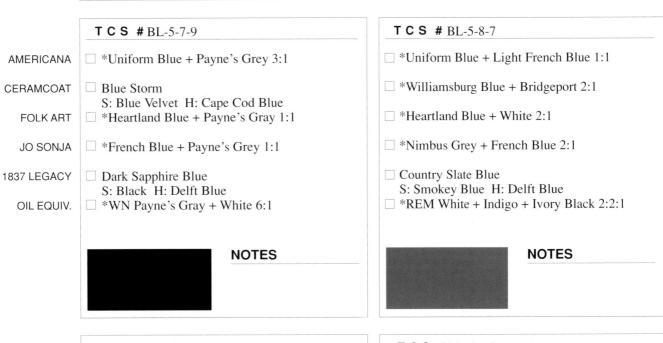

BRAND   COLOR   COLOR

TCS # BL-6-1-3

AMERICANA   ☐ *White + True Blue 4:1

CERAMCOAT   ☐ Blue Danube
                  S: Copen Blue H: Blue Mist

FOLK ART   ☐ *Light Blue + Patina (T)

JO SONJA   ☐ *White + Cobalt Blue Hue 3:1

1837 LEGACY   ☐ Gentle Blue
                  S: Blue Birds H: Snowball

OIL EQUIV.   ☐ *WN White + Cerulean Blue +
                  French Ultramarine 4:2:1

NOTES

ì ı / BL-6-1-5

☐ *True Blue + White 1:1

☐ Ocean Reef Blue
     S: Navy Blue H: Blue Danube

☐ *Cerulean Blue + Cobalt 3:1

☐ *Ultramarine Blue + White 1:1

☐ Tory Blue
     S: Manganese Blue H: Gentle Blue

☐ *WN Cerulean Blue + French Ultramarine +
     White 3:2:1

NOTES

TCS #BL-6-1-6

AMERICANA   ☐ *True Blue + Victorian Blue (T)

CERAMCOAT   ☐ Copen Blue
                  S: Opaque Blue H: Blue Danube

FOLK ART   ☐ Cobalt (AP)
                  S: Midnight H: Light Blue

JO SONJA   ☐ *Cobalt Blue Hue + Ultramarine Blue 1:1

1837 LEGACY   ☐ Sapphire Blue
                  S: Blazer Blue H: Gentle Blue

OIL EQUIV.   ☐ ARC Cerulean Blue Hue,
                  WN Ultramarine Green Shade

NOTES

TCS # BL-6-1-8

☐ *Ultra Blue Deep + Navy 3:1

☐ *Pthalo Blue + Navy 3:1

☐ *Cobalt + Brilliant Ultramarine 3:1

☐ Cobalt Blue Hue

☐ *Electric Blue + Thalo Blue 2:1

☐ ARC Cobalt Blue,
     REM Cobalt Blue Light,
     WN Cobalt Blue

NOTES

TCS # BL-7-2-8

AMERICANA   ☐ Midnite Blue
                  S: Payne's Grey H: Sapphire

CERAMCOAT   ☐ Manganese Blue
                  S: Black H: Wedgewood Blue

FOLK ART   ☐ Cerulean Blue (AP)
                  S: Thunder Blue H: Coastal Blue

JO SONJA   ☐ *Pthalo Blue + Storm Blue 2:1

1837 LEGACY   ☐ Manganese Blue
                  S: Kohl Blue H: Gentle Blue

OIL EQUIV.   ☐ WN Prussian Blue

NOTES

TCS # BL-7-2-9

☐ Navy Blue
     S: Payne's Grey H: Sapphire

☐ Prussian Blue
     S: Payne's Grey H: Salem Blue

☐ *Cobalt + Viridian 4:1

☐ *Pthalo Blue + Pthalo Green 4:1

☐ Prussian Blue
     S: Black H: Sapphire Blue

☐ REM Indigo Extra

NOTES

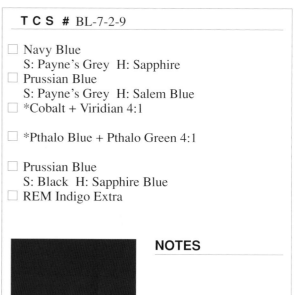

T C S # BL-7-4-3

AMERICANA	☐ Soft Blue S: Colonial Green H: Blue Chiffon
CERAMCOAT	☐ *Ocean Mist Blue + White + Chambray 2:2:1
FOLK ART	☐ *Icy White + Summer Sky 6:1
JO SONJA	☐ *White + Prussian Blue + Antique Green 16:1:1
1837 LEGACY	☐ *Sky Blue + Wedgewood Blue + White + Orange 3:1:1:T
OIL EQUIV.	☐ *REM White + Indigo Extra + GRUM Greenish Umber 20:2:1

NOTES

T C S # BL-7-4-8

AMERICANA	☐ Wedgewood Blue S: Deep Midnight Blue H: Sapphire
CERAMCOAT	☐ Blueberry S: Midnight Blue H: Ocean Reef Blue
FOLK ART	☐ *Thunder Blue + White 6:1
JO SONJA	☐ *Prussian Blue + White 4:1
1837 LEGACY	☐ *Thalo Blue + Pacifica 2:1
OIL EQUIV.	☐ *WN Prussian Blue + White 4:1

NOTES

T C S # BL-7-4-9

AMERICANA	☐ Blueberry S: Deep Midnight Blue H: Sapphire
CERAMCOAT	☐ *Navy Blue + Black (T)
FOLK ART	☐ Thunder Blue S: Licorice H: Light Blue
JO SONJA	☐ *Storm Blue + Sapphire 2:1
1837 LEGACY	☐ *Blazer Blue + Black (T)
OIL EQUIV.	☐ *WN Prussian Blue + Burnt Umber 1:1

NOTES

T C S # BG-1-3-2

AMERICANA	☐ *Salem Blue + Buttermilk 2:1
CERAMCOAT	☐ Salem Blue S: Blue Haze H: Blue Mist
FOLK ART	☐ *Azure Blue + Buttercream 1:1
JO SONJA	☐ *Colony Blue + Warm White 1:1
1837 LEGACY	☐ Big Sky S: Cool Blue H: Snowball
OIL EQUIV.	☐ *WN White + Viridian + REM Indigo Extra 6:3:1

NOTES

T C S # BG-1-3-3

AMERICANA	☐ Salem Blue S: Desert Turquoise H: Sea Aqua
CERAMCOAT	☐ Salem Blue (L) S: Blue Haze H: Blue Mist
FOLK ART	☐ *White + Azure Blue 4:1
JO SONJA	☐ *White + Colony Blue 4:1
1837 LEGACY	☐ Big Sky (L) S: Cool Blue H: Snowball
OIL EQUIV.	☐ *WN White + Viridian + REM Indigo Extra 6:3:1

NOTES

T C S # BG-1-3-8

AMERICANA	☐ Victorian Blue S: Midnight Blue H: Victorian Blue + White 1:1
CERAMCOAT	☐ *Manganese Blue + White 1:1
FOLK ART	☐ Blue Ribbon S: Thunder Blue H: Light Blue
JO SONJA	☐ *Sapphire + Ultra Blue Deep + Pthalo Green 3:1:1
1837 LEGACY	☐ *Manganese + White 1:1
OIL EQUIV.	☐ PRI Cerulean Blue Hue, WN Cerulean Blue

NOTES

BRAND **COLOR** **COLOR**

T C S # BG-1-4-2

AMERICANA	☐ *Salem Blue + Ice Blue 3:1
CERAMCOAT	☐ Ocean Mist Blue S: Colonial Blue H: Blue Mist
FOLK ART	☐ Sky Blue S: Bluebell H: Icy White
JO SONJA	☐ *Warm White + Storm Blue 15:1
1837 LEGACY	☐ *Big Sky + Atlantic Surf 1:1
OIL EQUIV.	☐ *WN White + Naples Yellow Light + Cerulean Blue 3:2:1

NOTES

T C S # BG-1-7-2

AMERICANA	☐ Blue Mist S: Colonial Green H: Ice Blue
CERAMCOAT	☐ Blue Wisp S: Blue Haze H: Light Sage
FOLK ART	☐ *Summer Sky + Gray Mist 2:1
JO SONJA	☐ *Smoked Pearl + Sapphire (T)
1837 LEGACY	☐ Atlantic Surf S: Fundy Blue H: White
OIL EQUIV.	☐ *WN White + French Ultramarine + Prussian Blue + Cad. Yellow Pale + Bt. Umber 30:2:1:1:2

NOTES

T C S #BG-1-7-3

AMERICANA	☐ Colonial Green (D) S: Teal Green H: Blue Mist
CERAMCOAT	☐ Blue Wisp (L) S: Blue Haze H: Light Sage
FOLK ART	☐ Summer Sky S: Teal Green H: White
JO SONJA	☐ *Smoked Pearl + Teal Green (T)
1837 LEGACY	☐ Atlantic Surf (L) S: Fundy Blue H: White
OIL EQUIV.	☐ *WN White + Fr. Ultramar. + Pruss. Blue + Cad. Yel. Pale + Bt. Umber 20:2:1:1:1

NOTES

T C S # BG-1-7-4

AMERICANA	☐ Colonial Green S: Teal Green H: Blue Mist
CERAMCOAT	☐ Blue Haze (D) S: Norsk Blue H: Blue Wisp
FOLK ART	☐ Summer Sky (L) S: Teal Green H: White
JO SONJA	☐ *Smoked Pearl + Teal Green 5:1
1837 LEGACY	☐ Fundy Blue (D) S: Eucalyptus H: Atlantic Surf
OIL EQUIV.	☐ *WN White + GRUM Greenish Umber + REM Turquoise Blue 8:2:1

NOTES

T C S #BG-1-7-5

AMERICANA	☐ *Blue Haze + White 1:1
CERAMCOAT	☐ Blue Haze S: Norsk Blue H: Blue Wisp
FOLK ART	☐ *Bluebell + Teal Green 2:1
JO SONJA	☐ *Nimbus + Teal + Storm Blue 4:1:1
1837 LEGACY	☐ Fundy Blue S: Eucalyptus H: Atlantic Surf
OIL EQUIV.	☐ *WN Cerulean Blue + REM Warm Grey + White 4:2:1

NOTES

T C S #BG-1-7-7

AMERICANA	☐ *Blue Haze + Victorian Blue 1:1
CERAMCOAT	☐ *Norsk Blue + Blue Haze 1:1
FOLK ART	☐ Bluebonnet S: Indigo H: Icy White
JO SONJA	☐ *Colony Blue + Nimbus Grey 2:1
1837 LEGACY	☐ *Nordic Blue + Fundy Blue 1:1
OIL EQUIV.	☐ *WN White + French Ultramarine + Burnt Umber + Prussian Blue 4:2:2:1

NOTES

	TCS # BG-1-7-8	**TCS # BG-2-4-5**
AMERICANA	☐ *Blue Haze + Blue/Grey Mist (T)	☐ *Indian Turquoise + Desert Turquoise 1:1
CERAMCOAT	☐ Norsk Blue S: Blue Spruce H: Blue Wisp	☐ Aquamarine S: Avalon Blue H: Salem Blue
FOLK ART	☐ *Bluebonnet + Medium Gray 6:1	☐ *White + Azure Blue 4:1
JO SONJA	☐ *White + Storm Blue + Gold Oxide 4:2:1	☐ *Colony Blue + White 1:1
1837 LEGACY	☐ Nordic Blue S: Slate Blue H: Aqua	☐ *Pacifica + White 2:1
OIL EQUIV.	☐ *REM Warm Grey + WN Cerulean Blue + White 4:2:1	☐ *WN Cerulean Blue + Viridian + White + REM Warm Grey 5:3:2:1

NOTES

NOTES

	TCS # BG-2-4-7	**TCS # BG-2-4-8**
AMERICANA	☐ *Desert Turquoise + Victorian Blue 2:1	☐ Blue Haze (D) S: Blue Green H: Desert Turquoise
CERAMCOAT	☐ Avalon Blue S: Prussian Blue H: Salem Blue	☐ Avalon Blue (L) S: Prussian Blue H: Salem Blue
FOLK ART	☐ *Azure Blue + Bluebonnet 3:1	☐ Bavarian Blue (Disc.) or * Bluebonnet + Azure Blue 1:1
JO SONJA	☐ Colony Blue	☐ *Warm White + Storm Blue + Gold Oxide 4:4:1
1837 LEGACY	☐ Pacifica S: Eucalyptus H: Cool Blue	☐ Pacifica (L) S: Eucalyptus H: Cool Blue
OIL EQUIV.	☐ ARC Pthalo Turquoise	☐ *WN Prussian Blue + Burnt Umber + White 1:1:3

NOTES

NOTES

	TCS # BG-2-4-9	**TCS # BG-3-1-6**
AMERICANA	☐ Blue Haze S: Blue Green H: Desert Turquoise	☐ *Desert Turquoise + Blue Green 6:1
CERAMCOAT	☐ *Blue Spruce + Colonial Blue 3:1	☐ Azure Blue S: Manganese Blue H: Blue Danube
FOLK ART	☐ * Bluebonnet + Azure Blue 2:1	☐ Azure Blue S: Navy Blue H: Coastal Blue
JO SONJA	☐ *Storm Blue + Warm White + Gold Oxide 1:1:T or Jo Sonja Bkg Light Teal	☐ *Aqua + Ultramarine Blue 1:1
1837 LEGACY	☐ *Eucalyptus + St. Clair Blue 3:1	☐ *Tory Blue + Pacifica 1:1
OIL EQUIV.	☐ *WN Burnt Umber + Prussian Blue + White 3:2:5	☐ *WN Winsor Blue + Cadmium Yellow Pale + White 3:1:10

NOTES

NOTES

BRAND   **COLOR**   **COLOR**

T C S # BG-3-4-3

AMERICANA	☐ Indian Turquoise S: Desert Turquoise H: Sea Aqua
CERAMCOAT	☐ *Colonial Blue + White 2:1
FOLK ART	☐ *White + Azure Blue + Coastal Blue 3:1:1
JO SONJA	☐ *White + Aqua + Sapphire 3:1:1
1837 LEGACY	☐ Cool Blue S: St. Clair Blue H: Snowball
OIL EQUIV.	☐ *WN Cerulean Blue + White + Viridian 3:2:1

NOTES

T C S # BG-3-4-5

☐ *Indian Turquoise + Victorian Blue (T)	
☐ *Blue Heaven + Colonial Blue 1:1	
☐ Coastal Blue S: Thunder Blue H: White	
☐ *White + Aqua + Sapphire 2:1:1	
☐ *Heavenly Blue + St. Clair Blue 1:1	
☐ *WN Winsor Blue + Cadmium Yellow Pale + White 3:1:20	

NOTES

T C S # BG-4-1-2

AMERICANA	☐ *Sea Aqua + White + Bluegrass 1:1:T
CERAMCOAT	☐ Tropic Bay Blue S: Emerald Green H: Tropic Bay + White 1:1
FOLK ART	☐ *Patina + White 1:1
JO SONJA	☐ *White + Aqua 4:1
1837 LEGACY	☐ Aqua S: Glacial Lake H: Holly Hock
OIL EQUIV.	☐ *WN White + REM Turquoise Blue + Yellow Citron 20:8:1

NOTES

T C S # BG-4-1-3

☐ *Sea Aqua + Bluegrass 5:1	
☐ *Tropic Bay Blue + Turquoise 1:1	
☐ Patina S: Turquoise H: White	
☐ *White + Aqua + Yellow Light 3:2:1	
☐ *Aqua + Glacial Lake 1:1	
☐ *REM White + Viridian 2:1	

NOTES

T C S # BG-4-1-4

AMERICANA	☐ *Sea Aqua + Bluegrass 3:1
CERAMCOAT	☐ Turquoise S: Emerald Green H: Turquoise + White 1:1
FOLK ART	☐ *Patina + Turquoise (T)
JO SONJA	☐ *Aqua + Yellow Lt. + White 1:1:1
1837 LEGACY	☐ Glacial Lake S: Mountain Blue H: Aqua
OIL EQUIV.	☐ *REM Viridian + White 1:1

NOTES

T C S # BG-4-1-5

☐ *Desert Turquoise + Bluegrass Green 1:1	
☐ Laguna Blue S: Pthalo Green H: Tropic Bay Blue	
☐ Aqua (AP) S: Teal H: Patina	
☐ Aqua	
☐ Mountain Blue S: Pthalo Green H: Glacial Lake	
☐ ARC Cobalt Turquoise, REM Turquoise Blue	

NOTES

T C S # BG-4-1-7

AMERICANA	☐ *Blue Green + Sea Aqua 3:1
CERAMCOAT	☐ *Hunter Green + Emerald Green 2:1
FOLK ART	☐ Teal S: Wintergreen H: Patina
JO SONJA	☐ *Pthalo Green + Aqua 2:1
1837 LEGACY	☐ *Mountain Blue + Pthalo Green 2:1
OIL EQUIV.	☐ *REM Viridian + WN Prussian Blue + White 4:1:2

NOTES

T C S # BG-4-1-8

AMERICANA	☐ Blue Green S: Payne's Grey H: Bluegrass
CERAMCOAT	☐ *Hunter Green + Emerald Green 1:1
FOLK ART	☐ Teal (L) S: Wintergreen H: Aqua Bright
JO SONJA	☐ *Pthalo Green + Pthalo Blue 1:1
1837 LEGACY	☐ *Manganese Blue + Pthalo Green 3:1
OIL EQUIV.	☐ REM Blue Green, WN Phthalo Turquoise

NOTES

T C S # BG-4-2-8

AMERICANA	☐ *Blue Green + Antique Teal 3:1
CERAMCOAT	☐ Truly Teal S: Blue Velvet H: Emerald Green
FOLK ART	☐ *Cerulean Blue + Wintergreen 1:1
JO SONJA	☐ *Pthalo Green + Colony Blue 4:1
1837 LEGACY	☐ *Manganese Blue + Pthalo Green 1:1
OIL EQUIV.	☐ WN Cobalt Turquoise *REM Cobalt Blue Light + Blue Green + White 5:2:1

NOTES

T C S # BG-4-4-3

AMERICANA	☐ *Desert Turquoise + White 1:1
CERAMCOAT	☐ Caribbean Blue S: Aquamarine H: White
FOLK ART	☐ *Coastal Blue + Patina 1:1
JO SONJA	☐ *Aqua + Colony Blue + White 3:1:1
1837 LEGACY	☐ *St. Clair Blue + White 1:1
OIL EQUIV.	☐ *WN White + Cerulean Blue + Viridian 4:3:2

NOTES

T C S # BG-4-4-5

AMERICANA	☐ Desert Turquoise S: Blue Green H: Sea Aqua
CERAMCOAT	☐ Colonial Blue S: Avalon Blue H: Caribbean Blue
FOLK ART	☐ *Azure Blue + Patina 2:1
JO SONJA	☐ *Aqua + Colony Blue + White 2:2:1
1837 LEGACY	☐ St. Clair Blue S: Pacifica H: Cool Blue
OIL EQUIV.	☐ PRI Turquoise, *WN Cerulean Blue + Viridian + White 4:2:1

NOTES

T C S # BG-4-7-8

AMERICANA	☐ *Teal Green + Cool Neutral 1:1
CERAMCOAT	☐ Salem Green S: Woodland Night Green H: Cactus Green
FOLK ART	☐ *Teal Green + Bluebonnet 2:1
JO SONJA	☐ Antique Green
1837 LEGACY	☐ Foliage Green S: Black Green H: Cypress Green
OIL EQUIV.	☐ *WN Prussian Blue + Cadmium Yellow Pale + White + Scarlet Lake 2:2:2:1

NOTES

BRAND	COLOR	COLOR

TCS #BG-4-7-9

AMERICANA	☐ *Deep Teal + Teal Green 1:1
CERAMCOAT	☐ *Woodland Night Green + Blue Spruce 1:1
FOLK ART	☐ *Emerald Isle + Navy Blue 3:1
JO SONJA	☐ *Teal Green + Colony Blue 1:1
1837 LEGACY	☐ Hunter Green S: Black Green H: Emerald Green
OIL EQUIV.	☐ *REM Sap Green + Prussian Blue 2:1

NOTES

TCS # BG-5-1-6

☐ Bluegrass Green
   S: Viridian Green H: Sea Aqua
☐ Emerald Green
   S: Pthalo Green H: Tropic Bay Blue
☐ Turquoise
   S: Wintergreen H: White
☐ *Aqua + Pthalo Green 4:1

☐ *St. Clair Blue + Pthalo Green 3:1

☐ WN Viridian,
   *REM Viridian + White 2:1

NOTES

TCS #BG-5-1-8

AMERICANA	☐ *Bluegrass Green + Viridian Green 1:1
CERAMCOAT	☐ Mallard Green S: Black Green H: Jade Green
FOLK ART	☐ *Turquoise + Teal 1:1
JO SONJA	☐ *Aqua + Pthalo Green 1:1
1837 LEGACY	☐ Dark Evergreen S: Black Green H: Holly Hock
OIL EQUIV.	☐ *WN Viridian + Cerulean Blue 2:1

NOTES

TCS # BG-5-3-6

☐ *Bluegrass Green + Teal Green 1:1

☐ *Laguna Blue + Avalon Blue 1:1

☐ *Teal + Teal Green 1:1

☐ Celadon

☐ *Emeraude + Pthalo Green 2:1

☐ *GRUM Manganese Blue + WN Prussian Blue +
   Winsor Yellow + White 6:1:2:2

NOTES

TCS #BG-5-3-7

AMERICANA	☐ Teal Green S: Blue Green H: Desert Turquoise
CERAMCOAT	☐ *Avalon + Blue Spruce 2:1
FOLK ART	☐ *Teal + Bluebonnet 1:1
JO SONJA	☐ *Nimbus Gray + Teal Green 2:1
1837 LEGACY	☐ Cove Blue S: Eucalyptus H: Big Sky
OIL EQUIV.	☐ *REM Viridian + WN Prussian Blue + White 8:1:20

NOTES

TCS #BG-5-3-8

☐ Antique Teal
   S: Black Green H: Teal Green
☐ Blue Spruce (D)
   S: Black Green H: Rainforest
☐ *Teal Green + Wintergreen 1:1

☐ *Colony Blue + Teal 1:1

☐ Eucalyptus
   S: Velvet Night H: St. Clair Blue
☐ *WN Terre Verte + Viridian 3:1

NOTES

T C S # BG-5-3-9

AMERICANA	☐ Antique Teal (L) S: Black Green H: Teal Green
CERAMCOAT	☐ Blue Spruce S: Black Green H: Rainforest
FOLK ART	☐ *Wintergreen + Prussian Blue 4:1
JO SONJA	☐ *Colony Blue + Teal 1:1
1837 LEGACY	☐ Eucalyptus (L) S: Velvet Night H: St. Clair Blue
OIL EQUIV.	☐ *WN French Ultramarine + Cadmium Yellow Pale 3:2

NOTES

T C S # BG-5-7-6

	☐ *Teal Green + White 1:1
	☐ *Blue Spruce + White 1:1
	☐ Teal Green S: Wrought Iron H: White ☐ *Teal Green + White 1:1
	☐ *Eucalyptus + White 1:1
	☐ *WN Prussian Blue + Cadmium Yellow Pale + White + Scarlet Lake 2:2:3:1

NOTES

T C S # BG-7-1-2

AMERICANA	☐ *Sea Aqua + White 1:1
CERAMCOAT	☐ *Turquoise + Ivory 1:1
FOLK ART	☐ *Patina + White 1:1
JO SONJA	☐ *Aqua + Yellow Light 1:1
1837 LEGACY	☐ Holly Hock S: Glacial Lake H: Marshland
OIL EQUIV.	☐ *REM White + Turquoise + WN Winsor Yellow 10:2:1

NOTES

T C S # BG-7-1-3

	☐ Sea Aqua S: Bluegrass Green H: Sea Aqua + White 1:1 ☐ *Turquoise + Ivory 2:1
	☐ Pastel Green S: Tartan Green H: Mint Green ☐ *White + Aqua + Yellow Light 2:1:1
	☐ *Holly Hock + Glacial Lake 1:1
	☐ WN Cobalt Green

NOTES

T C S # BG-7-1-5

AMERICANA	☐ *White + Bluegrass Green 2:1
CERAMCOAT	☐ Light Jade Green S: Emerald Green H: Pale Mint Green
FOLK ART	☐ *White + Emerald Isle 3:1
JO SONJA	☐ *White + Pthalo Green 4:1
1837 LEGACY	☐ *Aqua + Pthalo Green 1:1
OIL EQUIV.	☐ *WN White + Viridian + Cadmium Yellow Light 8:4:1

NOTES

T C S # BG-7-1-6

	☐ *Bluegrass Green + White 1:1
	☐ Jade Green S: Pthalo Green H: Jade Green + White 1:1 ☐ *White + Emerald Isle 1:1
	☐ *White + Pthalo Green 1:1
	☐ *Pthalo Green + Aqua 2:1
	☐ WN Winsor Emerald, *REM Turquoise + Sap Green 4:1

NOTES

TCS # BG-7-4-3

AMERICANA	☐ *Colonial Green + Mint Julep 1:1
CERAMCOAT	☐ Oasis Green S: Heritage Green H: Pale Mint Green
FOLK ART	☐ *Mint Green + Teal 3:1
JO SONJA	☐ *White + Celadon 4:1
1837 LEGACY	☐ *White + Emeraude 4:1
OIL EQUIV.	☐ *REM White + Sap Green + Blue Green 2:1:1

NOTES

TCS # BG-7-4-5

AMERICANA	☐ *Colonial Green + Sea Aqua 1:1
CERAMCOAT	☐ Heritage Green S: Woodland Night Green H: Cactus Green
FOLK ART	☐ *Mint Green + Tartan Green 1:1
JO SONJA	☐ *Aqua + Jade 4:1
1837 LEGACY	☐ *Glacial Lake + Emeraude 1:1
OIL EQUIV.	☐ *WN White + Prussian Blue + Yellow Ochre 2:1:1

NOTES

TCS # BG-8-2-9

AMERICANA	☐ *Deep Teal + Viridian Green 1:1
CERAMCOAT	☐ *Woodland Night Green + Hunter Green 1:1
FOLK ART	☐ Emerald Isle S: Licorice H: Mint Green
JO SONJA	☐ *Pthalo Green + Teal Green 4:1
1837 LEGACY	☐ *Pthalo Green + Forest Night 2:1
OIL EQUIV.	☐ *REM Viridian + WN Prussian Green 10:1

NOTES

TCS # BG-8-6-1

AMERICANA	☐ *Mint Julep + Jade (T)
CERAMCOAT	☐ *Cactus Green + White 2:1
FOLK ART	☐ Mint Green S: Poetry Green H: White
JO SONJA	☐ *White + Jade 5:1
1837 LEGACY	☐ *Cypress Green + White 1:1
OIL EQUIV.	☐ *WN Prussian Blue + Cadmium Lemon + White 2:3:30

NOTES

TCS # BG-8-6-2

AMERICANA	☐ *Mint Julep + Jade 1:1
CERAMCOAT	☐ Cactus Green S: Salem Green H: Pale Mint Green
FOLK ART	☐ *Poetry Green + White 3:1
JO SONJA	☐ *White + Jade 2:1
1837 LEGACY	☐ Cypress Green S: Emeraude H: Marshland
OIL EQUIV.	☐ *WN Prussian Blue + Cadmium Lemon + White 2:3:24

NOTES

TCS # BG-8-6-4

AMERICANA	☐ *Teal Green + Colonial Green + White 1:1:1
CERAMCOAT	☐ Rainforest Green S: Blue Spruce H: Cactus Green
FOLK ART	☐ *Teal Green + Bluebonnet 3:1
JO SONJA	☐ *Smoked Pearl + Teal Green 10:1
1837 LEGACY	☐ Emeraude S: Hunter Green H: Holly Hock
OIL EQUIV.	☐ *WN White + Prussian Blue + Cadmium Yellow Pale + Scarlet Lake 4:2:2:1

NOTES

BRAND	COLOR	COLOR

T C S # BG-8-8-1

AMERICANA	☐ *Silver Sage Green + White 1:1
CERAMCOAT	☐ Light Sage S: Silver Pine H: White
FOLK ART	☐ *Ice Blue + Poetry Green 2:1
JO SONJA	☐ *White + Smoked Pearl + Jade 2:2:1
1837 LEGACY	☐ *Antique Lace + Emeraude 6:1
OIL EQUIV.	☐ *WN White + Naples Yellow + French Ultramarine 8:2:1

NOTES

T C S # BG-8-8-3

AMERICANA	☐ Silver Sage Green S: Green Mist H: Dove Grey
CERAMCOAT	☐ Silver Pine S: Rainforest Green H: Light Sage
FOLK ART	☐ *Ice Blue + Poetry Green 2:1
JO SONJA	☐ *White + Smoked Pearl + Jade 1:1:1
1837 LEGACY	☐ *Jasper + Pelican 2:1
OIL EQUIV.	☐ *WN Naples Yellow + French Ultramarine + White 2:1:1

NOTES

T C S # BG-9-1-8

AMERICANA	☐ Viridian Green S: Payne's Grey H: Bluegrass Green
CERAMCOAT	☐ Phthalo Green S: Black Green H: Light Jade Green
FOLK ART	☐ *Emerald Isle + Kelly Green 1:1
JO SONJA	☐ Pthalo Green
1837 LEGACY	☐ Pthalo Green S: Black Green H: Glacial Lake
OIL EQUIV.	☐ ARC Pthalo Green (Yellow Shade), REM Viridian, WN Winsor Green

NOTES

T C S # BG-9-1-9

AMERICANA	☐ Viridian Green (L) S: Payne's Grey H: Bluegrass
CERAMCOAT	☐ Phthalo Green (L) S: Black Green H: Light Jade
FOLK ART	☐ *Wintergreen + Forest Green 1:1
JO SONJA	☐ *Pthalo Green + Hooker's Green 1:1
1837 LEGACY	☐ *Pthalo Green + Hunter Green 4:1
OIL EQUIV.	☐ ARC Pthalo Green

NOTES

T C S # BG-9-6-8

AMERICANA	☐ Deep Teal (D) S: Viridian Green H: Bluegrass Green
CERAMCOAT	☐ Alpine Green S: Deep River Green H: Cactus Green
FOLK ART	☐ Tartan Green S: Wrought Iron H: Buttercream
JO SONJA	☐ *Jade + Ultra Blue 4:1
1837 LEGACY	☐ *Hedge Row + Forest Night 2:1
OIL EQUIV.	☐ WN Cobalt Green Deep

NOTES

T C S # BG-9-6-9

AMERICANA	☐ Deep Teal S: Viridian Green H: Bluegrass Green
CERAMCOAT	☐ Woodland Night Green S: Black Green H: Jade Green
FOLK ART	☐ Wintergreen S: Licorice H: Summer Sky
JO SONJA	☐ *Teal Green + White (T) or Jo Sonja Bkg Victorian Green
1837 LEGACY	☐ Forest Night S: Hunter Green H: Cypress Green
OIL EQUIV.	☐ ARC Permanent Viridian Hue, PRI Phthalo Green

NOTES

BRAND   **COLOR**   **COLOR**

T C S # BG-9-7-6

AMERICANA	☐ *Deep Teal + Olive Green 2:1
CERAMCOAT	☐ *Woodland Night Green + Green Sea 1:1
FOLK ART	☐ Aspen Green S: Wrought Iron H: Tapioca
JO SONJA	☐ *Moss Green + Teal 2:1
1837 LEGACY	☐ *Emeraude + Algonquin Green 2:1
OIL EQUIV.	☐ *WN Olive Green + Prussian Blue + White 3:1:5

NOTES

T C S # BG-9-7-9

AMERICANA	☐ *Hauser Green Dark + Deep Teal 1:1
CERAMCOAT	☐ Dark Foliage Green S: Black Green H: Medium Foliage Green
FOLK ART	☐ Hauser Green Dark (AP) S: Wrought Iron H: Hauser Green Medium
JO SONJA	☐ Teal Green
1837 LEGACY	☐ *Hunter Green + Black Green 3:1
OIL EQUIV.	☐ ARC Forest Green

NOTES

T C S # GR-1-4-1

AMERICANA	☐ *White + Mint Julep 6:1
CERAMCOAT	☐ Pale Mint Green S: Village Green H: White
FOLK ART	☐ *White + Bayberry 6:1
JO SONJA	☐ *White + Brilliant Green 10:1
1837 LEGACY	☐ Marshland S: Jasper H: White
OIL EQUIV.	☐ *REM White + Sap Green 1:T

NOTES

T C S # GR-3-2-4

AMERICANA	☐ Kelly Green S: Dark Pine H: Bright Green
CERAMCOAT	☐ Spring Green S: Hunter Green H: Pale Mint Green
FOLK ART	☐ Kelly Green S: Wrought Iron H: White
JO SONJA	☐ *Brilliant Green + Aqua 1:1
1837 LEGACY	☐ *Erin Green + Glacial Lake 3:1
OIL EQUIV.	☐ WN Permanent Green

NOTES

T C S # GR-3-3-3

AMERICANA	☐ Mint Julep Green S: Green Mist H: White 1:1
CERAMCOAT	☐ *White + Christmas Green 6:1
FOLK ART	☐ *White + Shamrock 6:1
JO SONJA	☐ *White + Jade 4:1
1837 LEGACY	☐ *White + Chrome Green Light 2:1
OIL EQUIV.	☐ *REM White + Sap Green 4:1

NOTES

T C S # GR-3-3-5

AMERICANA	☐ Holly Green S: Hauser Dark Green H: Bright Green
CERAMCOAT	☐ *Green Isle + Pthalo Green 2:1
FOLK ART	☐ *Evergreen + Emerald Isle 1:1
JO SONJA	☐ *Brilliant Green + Pthalo Green 2:1 or Jo Sonja Bkg Holiday Green
1837 LEGACY	☐ *Erin Green + Pthalo Green 2:1
OIL EQUIV.	☐ WN Winsor Green (Yellow Shade), *REM Sap Green + WN Viridian + White 4:2:1

NOTES

TCS # GR-3-3-6

AMERICANA	☐ Dark Pine S: Black Forest Green H: Bluegrass Green
CERAMCOAT	☐ *Christmas Green + Pthalo Green 1:1
FOLK ART	☐ *Shamrock + Tartan Green 1:1
JO SONJA	☐ *Teal Green + Moss Green 1:1
1837 LEGACY	☐ Hedge Row S: Hunter Green H: Cypress Green
OIL EQUIV.	☐ *REM Sap Green + WN Viridian + White 5:2:1

NOTES

TCS # GR-3-5-5

| ☐ *Pine Green + White 2:1 |
| ☐ *Hunter Green + White 2:1 |
| ☐ Leaf Green
S: Green Forest H: Spring White |
| ☐ *White + Brill. Green + Pthalo Green 2:1:1 |
| ☐ *1837 Green + Pthalo Green + White 2:2:1 |
| ☐ *WN Pruss.Blue + Fr. Ultram. + Cad. Lemon +
Cad. Yel. Pale + White 1:1:1:1:4 |

NOTES

TCS # GR-3-5-7

AMERICANA	☐ *Forest Green + Leaf Green 1:1
CERAMCOAT	☐ Deep River Green (D) S: Black Green H: Cactus Green
FOLK ART	☐ Shamrock S: Wrought Iron H: Warm White
JO SONJA	☐ *Teal Green + Brilliant Green + Raw Sienna 1:1:T
1837 LEGACY	☐ *Forest Green + Holly Green 1:1
OIL EQUIV.	☐ WN Oxide of Chromium

NOTES

TCS # GR-3-5-8

| ☐ Black Forest Green
S: Black H: Dark Pine |
| ☐ Deep River Green
S: Black Green H: Cactus Green |
| ☐ Green Forest
S: Wrought Iron H: Leaf Green |
| ☐ Hooker's Green |
| ☐ *Forest Night + Hunter Green 1:1 |
| ☐ *WN Prussian Blue + Olive Green +
Sap Green 1:1:1 |

NOTES

TCS # GR-3-6-8

AMERICANA	☐ Hauser Dark Green S: Black H: Hauser Medium Green
CERAMCOAT	☐ Hunter Green S: Black Green H: Light Jade Green
FOLK ART	☐ Hunter Green S: Wrought Iron H: White
JO SONJA	☐ *Teal Green + Raw Sienna (T)
1837 LEGACY	☐ *Erin Green + Hunter Green 3:1
OIL EQUIV.	☐ WN Prussian Green

NOTES

TCS # GR-3-7-3

| ☐ *Jade Green + White 1:1 |
| ☐ Village Green
S: Green Sea H: Pale Mint Green |
| ☐ *Poetry Green + White 1:1 |
| ☐ *White + Jade 3:1 |
| ☐ Myrtle Green
S: Jasper H: Marshland |
| ☐ *REM White + Indigo Extra +
WN Winsor Yellow 20:2:1 |

NOTES

BRAND	COLOR	COLOR

T C S # GR-3-7-4

AMERICANA	☐ Green Mist S: Deep Teal H: Mint Julep Green
CERAMCOAT	☐ *Green Sea + Rainforest (T)
FOLK ART	☐ Poetry Green S: Licorice H: Teal Green
JO SONJA	☐ *Jade + White (T)
1837 LEGACY	☐ Jasper S: Hedge Row H: Myrtle Green
OIL EQUIV.	☐ *WN White + Cadmium Lemon + Prussian Blue 16:3:2

NOTES

T C S # GR-3-7-5

☐ Arbor Green S: Dark Pine H: Mint Julep Green
☐ *Green Sea + Rainforest 2:1
☐ *Poetry Green + Shamrock 2:1
☐ *Jade + Green Oxide + Prussian Blue 2:1:T
☐ *Hedge Row + Jasper 3:1
☐ *WN White + Yellow Ochre + Prussian Blue 10:4:1

NOTES

T C S # GR-3-8-4

AMERICANA	☐ *Green Mist + Shale Green 1:1
CERAMCOAT	☐ *Stonewedge Green + Wedgewood Green 1:1
FOLK ART	☐ Italian Sage S: Aspen Green H: Mint Green
JO SONJA	☐ *Jade Green + Nimbus Grey 1:1
1837 LEGACY	☐ *Jasper + Sage 3:1
OIL EQUIV.	☐ *WN White + Raw Sienna + GRUM Greenish Umber 10:4:1

NOTES

T C S # GR-4-6-5

☐ *Jade + Forest Green 3:1
☐ Leprechaun S: Christmas Green H: Village Green
☐ Mystic Green S: Wrought Iron H: Tapioca
☐ Jade
☐ Blarney S: Algonquin Green H: Sage
☐ *WN White + Cadmium Lemon + Prussian Blue 9:3:2

NOTES

T C S # GR-5-1-1

AMERICANA	☐ *White + Holly Green (T)
CERAMCOAT	☐ Eggshell White S: Village Green H: White
FOLK ART	☐ Spring White S: Bayberry H: White
JO SONJA	☐ *White + Brilliant Green (T)
1837 LEGACY	☐ *White + Erin Green (T)
OIL EQUIV.	☐ *WN White + Chrome Green 30:1

NOTES

T C S # GR-5-1-5

☐ *Mistletoe + Leaf Green 1:1
☐ Green Isle S: Hunter Green H: Kelly Green
☐ *Shamrock + Fresh Foliage 4:1
☐ *Brilliant Green + Teal Green 3:1
☐ *Erin Green + Holly Green 8:1
☐ *SHIV Yellow Citron + GRUM Thalo Green 6:2

NOTES

T C S # GR-5-3-8

AMERICANA	☐ Midnite Green S: Black Green H: Forest Green
CERAMCOAT	☐ *Deep River Green + Christmas Green 1:1
FOLK ART	☐ *Thicket + Shamrock 1:1
JO SONJA	☐ *Teal Green + Raw Sienna 2:1
1837 LEGACY	☐ *Bay Leaf + Black Green 1:1
OIL EQUIV.	☐ REM Greenish Umber

NOTES

T C S # GR-5-3-9

☐ Black Green
S: Lamp (Ebony) Black H: Forest Green
☐ Black Green
S: None H: Blue Haze
☐ Wrought Iron
S: Licorice H: Bayberry
☐ *Teal Green + Black 3:1 or
Jo Sonja Bkg Forest Green
☐ Black Green
S: Black H: Moss
☐ GRUM Greenish Umber, *WN Raw Umber +
Burnt Umber + Fr. Ultramarine + White 2:1:1:1

NOTES

T C S # GR-5-4-6

AMERICANA	☐ *Jade Green + Kelly Green 4:1
CERAMCOAT	☐ Green Sea S: Chrome Green Light H: Village Green
FOLK ART	☐ *White + Grass Green 1:1
JO SONJA	☐ *Jade + Moss Green 6:1
1837 LEGACY	☐ Prairie Green S: Irish Green H: Myrtle Green
OIL EQUIV.	☐ WN Terre Verte

NOTES

T C S # GR-5-4-7

☐ Leaf Green
S: Hauser Dark Green H: Mistletoe
☐ Christmas Green
S: Hunter Green H: Kelly Green
☐ *Shamrock + Evergreen 1:1
☐ *Brilliant Green + Teal 6:1
☐ Holly Green
S: Hunter Green H: Emerald Green
☐ WN Chrome Green Deep Hue

NOTES

T C S # GR-5-6-4

AMERICANA	☐ Jade Green S: Light Avocado H: Jade Green + White 1:1
CERAMCOAT	☐ Wedgewood Green S: Forest Green H: Sea Grass
FOLK ART	☐ Bayberry S: Thicket H: White
JO SONJA	☐ *Nimbus Grey + Jade + Moss Green 1:1:1
1837 LEGACY	☐ Wedgewood Green S: Algonquin Green H: Myrtle Green
OIL EQUIV.	☐ *WN Ultramarine Blue+ Cadmium Yellow Pale + White 1:1:6

NOTES

T C S # GR-6-2-5

☐ *Holly Green + Bright Green 1:1
☐ *Jubilee Green + Green Isle 1:1
☐ *Evergreen + Fresh Foliage 4:1
☐ *Brilliant Green + Pthalo Green (T)
☐ Erin Green
S: Pthalo Green H: Clover Green
☐ WN Permanent Green Light

NOTES

COLOR	**COLOR**

T C S # GR-6-4-5

AMERICANA	☐ Mistletoe
	S: Forest Green H: Bright Green
CERAMCOAT	☐ Kelly Green
	S: Christmas Green H: Apple Green
FOLK ART	☐ Evergreen
	S: Southern Pine H: White
JO SONJA	☐ *Brilliant Green + Green Oxide 1:1
1837 LEGACY	☐ Irish Green
	S: Forest Night H: Lime
OIL EQUIV.	☐ REM Emerald Green

NOTES

T C S # GR-6-6-6

☐ Forest Green
S: Hauser Dark Green H: Mistletoe
☐ *Chrome Green Light + Forest Green 1:1
☐ Green Meadow
S: Licorice H: Basil Green
☐ *Green Oxide + Pine Green 6:1
☐ *Chrome Green Light + Algonquin Green 1:1
☐ *WN Olive Green + Sap Green + Prussian Blue 2:2:1

NOTES

T C S # GR-7-2-5

AMERICANA	☐ *Bright Green + Kelly Green 1:1
CERAMCOAT	☐ Jubilee Green
	S: Christmas Green H: Apple Green
FOLK ART	☐ *Evergreen + Fresh Foliage 1:1
JO SONJA	☐ Brilliant Green
1837 LEGACY	☐ Emerald Green
	S: Holly Green H: Lime
OIL EQUIV.	☐ WN Cadmium Green

NOTES

T C S # GR-7-3-5

☐ *Mistletoe + Green Olive 4:1
☐ *Kelly Green + Leaf Green 2:1
☐ Grass Green
S: Shamrock H: Warm White
☐ *Green Oxide + Moss Green 3:1
☐ *Irish Green + 1837 Green 2:1
☐ *WN Sap Green + Cadmium Lemon + White 4:1:5

NOTES

T C S # GR-7-4-5

AMERICANA	☐ Hauser Medium Green
	S: Hauser Dark Green H: Hauser Light Green
CERAMCOAT	☐ Medium Foliage Green
	S: Dark Foliage Green H: Light Foliage Green
FOLK ART	☐ Hauser Medium Green (AP)
	S: Hauser Dark Green H: Hauser Light Green
JO SONJA	☐ Sap Green
1837 LEGACY	☐ *Chrome Green Light + Moss 1:1
OIL EQUIV.	☐ ARC Permanent Sap Green, PRI Sap Green

NOTES

T C S # GR-7-7-2

☐ Soft Sage
S: Jade Green H: White
☐ *Village Green + White + Sea Grass 1:1:1
☐ *White + Basil Green 2:1
☐ *White + Green Oxide + Cadmium Yellow Mid 10:1:T
☐ *Myrtle + White 1:1
☐ *REM Brilliant Yellow Lt. + Yellow Ochre + GRUM Greenish Umber 15:1:1

NOTES

TCS #GR-7-7-4

AMERICANA	☐ *Olive Green + Light Avocado 4:1
CERAMCOAT	☐ *Wedgewood Green + Lima Green 3:1
FOLK ART	☐ Basil Green S: Southern Pine H: Warm White
JO SONJA	☐ *Moss Green + Jade 2:1
1837 LEGACY	☐ *Sage + 1837 Green 3:1
OIL EQUIV.	☐ *WN White + Sap Green + Cadmium Scarlet 5:1:T

NOTES

TCS # GR-7-8-4

AMERICANA	☐ Shale Green S: Light Avocado H: Cool Neutral Toning
CERAMCOAT	☐ *Stonewedge + Lichen Grey 2:1
FOLK ART	☐ Gray Green S: Dapple Gray H: Gray Mist
JO SONJA	☐ *Smoked Pearl + Nimbus Grey 2:1
1837 LEGACY	☐ *Sage + Sterling Grey 1:1
OIL EQUIV.	☐ *WN White + Olive Green 3:1

NOTES

TCS #GR-7-9-4

AMERICANA	☐ Celery Green S: Avocado H: Limeade
CERAMCOAT	☐ Stonewedge Green S: English Yew Green H: Eggshell White
FOLK ART	☐ *Basil Green + Southern Pine 6:1
JO SONJA	☐ *Skintone + Pine Green 3:1
1837 LEGACY	☐ Sage S: Algonquin Green H: Myrtle Green
OIL EQUIV.	☐ *WN White + Cadmium Yellow Pale + Ultramarine Blue + Burnt Umber 10:2:1:1

NOTES

TCS # GR-8-2-3

AMERICANA	☐ *Bright Green + Yellow Light 2:1
CERAMCOAT	☐ *Lime Green + Luscious Lemon 2:1
FOLK ART	☐ *Green + Sunny Yellow 1:1
JO SONJA	☐ *Yellow Light + Brilliant Green 3:1
1837 LEGACY	☐ Clover Green S: Holly Green H: Spring Green
OIL EQUIV.	☐ *SHIV Yellow Citron + GRUM Thalo Green 4:1

NOTES

TCS #GR-8-2-4

AMERICANA	☐ Bright Green S: Forest Green H: Bright Green + White 1:1
CERAMCOAT	☐ Lime Green S: Kelly Green H: Lima Green
FOLK ART	☐ Green S: Shamrock H: White
JO SONJA	☐ Green Light
1837 LEGACY	☐ Lime S: Emerald Green H: Spring Green
OIL EQUIV.	☐ ARC Permanent Green Light

NOTES

TCS #GR-8-3-9

AMERICANA	☐ *Black Forest Green + Evergreen 1:1
CERAMCOAT	☐ *Deep River Green + Black Green 1:1
FOLK ART	☐ Sap Green (AP) S: Wrought Iron H: Leaf Green
JO SONJA	☐ *Teal Green + Pine Green 2:1
1837 LEGACY	☐ *Pthalo Green + Hunter Green 1:1
OIL EQUIV.	☐ REM Sap Green

NOTES

COLOR	**COLOR**

T C S # GR-8-6-5

BRAND	
AMERICANA	☐ *Avocado + Evergreen 1:1
CERAMCOAT	☐ Chrome Green Light S: Dark Forest H: Green Sea
FOLK ART	☐ *Old Ivy + Clover 1:1
JO SONJA	☐ Green Oxide
1837 LEGACY	☐ Chrome Green Light S: Algonquin Green H: Myrtle Green
OIL EQUIV.	☐ ARC Chromium Green Oxide

NOTES

T C S # GR-8-6-6

AMERICANA	☐ *Avocado + Evergreen 2:1
CERAMCOAT	☐ Forest Green S: Dark Forest H: Leprechaun
FOLK ART	☐ Old Ivy S: Wrought Iron H: Bayberry
JO SONJA	☐ *Green Oxide + Pine Green (T)
1837 LEGACY	☐ Algonquin Green S: Black Green H: 1837 Green
OIL EQUIV.	☐ *WN Chrome Green + Ultramarine Blue + Burnt Umber + White 4:2:1:1

NOTES

T C S # GR-8-6-8

AMERICANA	☐ *Evergreen + Midnite Green 1:1
CERAMCOAT	☐ Pine Green S: Black Green H: Jubilee Green
FOLK ART	☐ *Thicket + Old Ivy 2:1
JO SONJA	☐ *Pine Green + Green Oxide + Payne's Grey 2:1:1
1837 LEGACY	☐ Evergreen S: Bay Leaf H: 1837 Green
OIL EQUIV.	☐ *WN Ivory Black + Cadmium Yellow Light 4:2

NOTES

T C S # YG-3-2-6

AMERICANA	☐ *Avocado + Yellow Green 1:1
CERAMCOAT	☐ Vibrant Green S: Dark Jungle H: Leaf Green
FOLK ART	☐ *Clover + Old Ivy 2:1
JO SONJA	☐ *Green Oxide + Yellow Light 1:1
1837 LEGACY	☐ Garland S: Ivy H: 1837 Green
OIL EQUIV.	☐ WN Sap Green

NOTES

T C S # YG-4-2-3

AMERICANA	☐ *Mistletoe + Bright Green 2:1
CERAMCOAT	☐ Leaf Green S: Seminole Green H: Lima Green
FOLK ART	☐ *Grass Green + Fresh Foliage 5:1
JO SONJA	☐ *Sap Green + Brilliant Green 2:1
1837 LEGACY	☐ *1837 Green + Clover Green 5:1
OIL EQUIV.	☐ *WN Winsor Yellow + REM Indigo Extra 4:1

NOTES

T C S # YG-4-3-2

AMERICANA	☐ *Cadmium Yellow + Leaf Green 6:1
CERAMCOAT	☐ *Leaf Green + Lima Green 3:1
FOLK ART	☐ Fresh Foliage S: Thicket H: Warm White
JO SONJA	☐ *Yellow Light + Green Oxide 4:1
1837 LEGACY	☐ Antique Green S: Garland H: Spring Green
OIL EQUIV.	☐ *WN White + Sap Green + Cadmium Lemon 5:2:1

NOTES

BRAND	COLOR	COLOR

T C S # YG-4-3-3

AMERICANA	☐ Hauser Light Green S: Hauser Medium Green H: Olive Green
CERAMCOAT	☐ Light Foliage Green S: Medium Foliage Green H: Lima Green
FOLK ART	☐ Hauser Light Green (AP) S: Hauser Medium Green H: Fresh Foliage
JO SONJA	☐ *Sap Green + Green Oxide 3:1
1837 LEGACY	☐ 1837 Green S: Moss H: Green Tea
OIL EQUIV.	☐ *WN White + Sap Green + Cadmium Lemon + Scarlet Lake 10:8:2:1

NOTES

T C S # YG-4-3-6

	☐ Avocado S: Evergreen H: Light Avocado
	☐ Seminole Green S: Dark Forest H: Leaf Green
	☐ Clover S: Shamrock H: Warm White
	☐ *Green Oxide + Brilliant Green 2:1
	☐ Moss S: Evergreen H: Antique Green
	☐ PRI Emerald Green

NOTES

T C S # YG-4-3-7

AMERICANA	☐ Evergreen S: Black H: Avocado
CERAMCOAT	☐ Dark Jungle Green S: Gamal Green H: Leaf Green
FOLK ART	☐ Olive Green S: Wrought Iron H: Fresh Foliage
JO SONJA	☐ Pine Green (D)
1837 LEGACY	☐ Shrub S: Bay Leaf H: Chrome Green Light
OIL EQUIV.	☐ REM Olive Green

NOTES

T C S # YG-4-3-8

	☐ *Evergreen + Plantation Pine 1:1
	☐ Dark Forest Green S: Black Green H: Seminole
	☐ Thicket S: Wrought Iron H: Basil Green
	☐ Pine Green
	☐ Ivy S: Black Green H: Moss
	☐ *WN Chrome Green + Ultramarine Blue + Burnt Umber 2:1:1

NOTES

T C S # YG-4-3-9

AMERICANA	☐ Plantation Pine S: Black Green H: Avocado
CERAMCOAT	☐ Gamal Green S: Black Green H: Seminole
FOLK ART	☐ Southern Pine S: Licorice H: Basil Green
JO SONJA	☐ *Pine Green + Black + Yellow Oxide 1:T:T
1837 LEGACY	☐ Bay Leaf S: Black H: Sage
OIL EQUIV.	☐ *WN Olive Green + Sap Green + White 4:2:1

NOTES

T C S # YG-4-4-9

	☐ *Plantation Pine + Burnt Umber 3:1
	☐ *English Yew + Burnt Umber 3:1
	☐ Green Umber (AP) S: Pure Black H: Hauser Medium Green
	☐ *Pine Green + Olive Green 1:1
	☐ *Ivy + Burnt Umber 3:1
	☐ *WN Burnt Umber + GRUM Thalo Green 6:1

NOTES

	COLOR		COLOR

TCS #YG-5-6-2

AMERICANA	☐ Olive Green S: Hauser Medium Green H: Yellow Light
CERAMCOAT	☐ *Leaf Green + White 1:1
FOLK ART	☐ *Fresh Foliage + Olive Green (T)
JO SONJA	☐ *Moss Green + White + Brilliant Green 5:2:1
1837 LEGACY	☐ *1837 Green + White 1:1
OIL EQUIV.	☐ *REM Olive Green + WN Lemon Yellow + White 4:2:1

NOTES

TCS # YG-5-6-5

AMERICANA	☐ Light Avocado S: Avocado H: Hauser Light Green
CERAMCOAT	☐ *English Yew + Apple Green 1:1
FOLK ART	☐ *Olive Green + Fresh Foliage 1:1
JO SONJA	☐ *Yellow Oxide + Pine Green + Nimbus Grey 1:1:1
1837 LEGACY	☐ *Green Olive + Green Tea 1:1
OIL EQUIV.	☐ *WN French Ultramarine + Cadmium Yellow Light + White 4:2:1

NOTES

TCS #YG-5-6-6

AMERICANA	☐ *Plantation Pine + Olive Green 1:1
CERAMCOAT	☐ *English Yew + Apple Green 2:1
FOLK ART	☐ *Olive Green + Southern Pine 2:1
JO SONJA	☐ *Nimbus Gray + Pine Green 2:1
1837 LEGACY	☐ Artichoke S: Shrub H: Light Yellow Green
OIL EQUIV.	☐ *WN Cad.Yel. Pale + Ultramarine Blue + Burnt Umber + White 2:2:2:1

NOTES

TCS # YG-5-6-7

AMERICANA	☐ *Plantation Pine + Avocado 4:1
CERAMCOAT	☐ English Yew Green S: Black Green H: Stonewedge
FOLK ART	☐ *Olive Green + Southern Pine 1:1
JO SONJA	☐ *Pine Green + Black (carbon) 12:1
1837 LEGACY	☐ Green Olive S: Olivette H: Light Yellow Green
OIL EQUIV.	☐ *REM Greenish Umber + WN Cadmium Yellow Light + White 4:2:1

NOTES

TCS #YG-6-2-3

AMERICANA	☐ *Olive Green + Lemon Yellow 1:1
CERAMCOAT	☐ Apple Green S: Seminole H: Pineapple Yellow
FOLK ART	☐ *Yellow Light + Fresh Foliage 1:1
JO SONJA	☐ *Yellow Light + Green Oxide 4:1
1837 LEGACY	☐ Green Tea S: Antique Green H: Maize
OIL EQUIV.	☐ *WN Lemon Yellow + White + REM Sap Green 6:2:1

NOTES

TCS # YG-7-3-2

AMERICANA	☐ Limeade S: Olive Green H: White
CERAMCOAT	☐ *White + Olive Green + Lima 4:1:1
FOLK ART	☐ Lime Yellow S: Olive Green H: White
JO SONJA	☐ *White + Moss Green + Cadmium Yellow Light + Pine Green 6:2:T:T
1837 LEGACY	☐ *Myrtle + Light Yellow Green + White 2:2:1
OIL EQUIV.	☐ REM Rembrandt Yellow

NOTES

YELLOW GREEN 5-6-2 / YELLOW GREEN 7-3-2

COLOR　　　　**COLOR**

T C S # YG-7-3-3

AMERICANA ☐ *Reindeer Moss + Olive Green 1:1

CERAMCOAT ☐ Sea Grass
　　　　　　S: Forest Green H: Lima Green

FOLK ART ☐ *Hauser Light Green + White 1:1

JO SONJA ☐ *Sap Green + Moss Green + White 1:1:1

1837 LEGACY ☐ *Canola + Wedgewood Green 1:1

OIL EQUIV. ☐ REM Rembrandt Yellow (L)

NOTES

T C S # YG-8-2-2

☐ Yellow Green
　S: Hauser Medium Green H: Yellow Light
☐ Lima Green
　S: Leaf Green H: Pineapple Yellow
☐ *Sunny Yellow + Fresh Foliage 2:1

☐ *Yellow Light + Brilliant Green 10:1

☐ Spring Green
　S: 1837 Green H: Canola
☐ REM Cinnabar Green,
　WN Cadmium Green Pale

NOTES

T C S # YG-8-8-3

AMERICANA ☐ Dried Basil Green
　　　　　　 S: Antique Green H: Cool Neutral

CERAMCOAT ☐ *Lichen Grey + Boston Fern 3:1

FOLK ART ☐ *Butter Pecan + Olive Green 3:1

JO SONJA ☐ *Moss Green + Territorial Beige +
　　　　　　 Nimbus Grey 2:2:1

1837 LEGACY ☐ *Olive Branch + Empire Green 10:1

OIL EQUIV. ☐ *WN White + Olive Green + Yellow Ochre 3:1:1

NOTES

T C S # YG-8-8-4

☐ *White + Antique Green 4:1

☐ Olive Yellow
　S: Avocado H: Pineapple Yellow
☐ *White + Olive Green + English Mustard 4:1:1

☐ *White + Yellow Oxide + Pine Green 4:2:1

☐ Olive Branch
　S: Empire Green H: Oatmeal
☐ *WN Raw Sienna + Yellow Ochre +
　SHIV Prussian Blue 6:4:1

NOTES

T C S # YG-8-8-7

AMERICANA ☐ Antique Green
　　　　　　 S: Plantation Pine H: Hauser Light Green

CERAMCOAT ☐ Boston Fern
　　　　　　 S: Gamal Green H: Antique Gold

FOLK ART ☐ *Olive Green + English Mustard 1:1

JO SONJA ☐ *Yellow Oxide + Pine Green 2:1

1837 LEGACY ☐ Empire Green
　　　　　　 S: Olivette H: Olive Branch

OIL EQUIV. ☐ *WN Olive Green + Cadmium Yellow 2:1

NOTES

T C S # YG-9-2-3

☐ *Antique Gold Deep + Hauser Light Green 12:1

☐ *Lime Green + Straw 1:1

☐ *Sunny Yellow + Fresh Foliage 2:1

☐ *Yellow Light + Moss Green 3:1

☐ Light Yellow Green
　S: Empire Green H: Barley
☐ *SHIV Yellow Citron + WN Yellow Ochre +
　White 6:2:1

NOTES

T C S # YG-9-2-4

AMERICANA   ☐ *Lemon Yellow + White + Olive Green + Calico Red 4:2:1:T

CERAMCOAT   ☐ *Bright Yellow + Lima Green + Napthol Crimson 1:1:T

FOLK ART   ☐ Lime Light
S: Hauser Green Light H: Buttercream

JO SONJA   ☐ *Yellow Light + Moss Green 4:1

1837 LEGACY   ☐ *Light Yellow Green + White 2:1

OIL EQUIV.   ☐ *SHIV Yellow Citron + WN White + Yellow Ochre 6:4:2

NOTES

T C S # YG-9-4-6

☐ Antique Gold Deep
S: Antique Green H: Olde Gold

☐ *Cloudberry Tan + Timberline 4:1

☐ *Olive Green + English Mustard 2:1

☐ *Moss Green + Yellow Oxide 1:1

☐ *Apache + Empire Green 4:1

☐ ARC Yellow Green

NOTES

T C S # YG-9-6-2

AMERICANA   ☐ *Olive Green + Antique Gold 3:1

CERAMCOAT   ☐ *Apple Green + Avocado 2:1

FOLK ART   ☐ *Olive Green + Yellow Ochre 1:1

JO SONJA   ☐ Moss Green

1837 LEGACY   ☐ *Empire Green + Antique Green 1:1

OIL EQUIV.   ☐ *SHIV Yell. Cit. + GRUM Bt. Sien. + WN Bt. Umber + GRUM Thalo Gr. + White 10:3:2:1:1

NOTES

T C S # YG-9-8-7

☐ *Antique Green + Antique Gold 2:1

☐ Avocado
S: Gamal Green H: Antique Gold

☐ *Olive Green + Teddy Bear Tan 1:1

☐ *Raw Sienna + Pine Green 1:1 or Jo Sonja Bkg Olive Green

☐ Olivette
S: Black H: Green Olive

☐ WN Olive Green

NOTES

T C S # YG-9-9-2

AMERICANA   ☐ Reindeer Moss Green
S: Light Avocado H: Cool Neutral

CERAMCOAT   ☐ *Light Timberline + White 2:1

FOLK ART   ☐ *White + Olive Green + Teddy Bear Tan 4:2:1

JO SONJA   ☐ *Smoked Pearl + Moss Green 2:1

1837 LEGACY   ☐ *White + Empire Green 2:1

OIL EQUIV.   ☐ *WN White + Olive Green + Cadmium Yellow Pale 4:1:1

NOTES

T C S # YG-9-9-3

☐ *Antique Green + Sand 1:1

☐ Light Timberline Green
S: Timberline Green H: Olive Yellow

☐ *White + Olive Green + Teddy Bear Tan 2:2:1

☐ *White + Pine Green + Yellow Oxide 1:1:1

☐ *White + Olive Branch + Green Olive 2:2:1

☐ WN Davy's Gray

NOTES

T C S # YG-9-9-7

AMERICANA	☐ *Plantation Pine + Pumpkin 5:1
CERAMCOAT	☐ Timberline 　　S: Burnt Umber H: Light Timberline
FOLK ART	☐ *Olive Green + Teddy Bear Tan 2:1
JO SONJA	☐ *Pine Green + Yellow Oxide + Vermillion 2:1:1
1837 LEGACY	☐ *Green Olive + Olivette 2:1
OIL EQUIV.	☐ *WN Olive Green + Cadmium Yellow 1:1

NOTES

T C S # YG-9-9-9

☐ *Plantation Pine + Black 2:1
☐ *Avocado + Black 2:1
☐ *Southern Pine + Black 2:1
☐ Olive Green
☐ *Green Olive + Pewter 1:1
☐ ARC Olive Green

NOTES

T C S # BR-1-2-2

AMERICANA	☐ Camel 　　S: Milk Chocolate H: Sand
CERAMCOAT	☐ *Flesh Tan + Dark Goldenrod 6:1
FOLK ART	☐ *Cappuccino + Buttercup 3:1
JO SONJA	☐ *Warm White + Raw Sienna + 　　Yellow Oxide 3:2:1
1837 LEGACY	☐ *Chamois + Tundra 6:1
OIL EQUIV.	☐ *WN Yellow Ochre + White 1:1

NOTES

T C S # BR-1-2-3

☐ *Cool Neutral + Milk Chocolate 2:1
☐ Palomino Tan 　　S: Spice Tan H: Old Parchment
☐ Teddy Bear Tan 　　S: Teddy Bear Brown H: Clay Bisque
☐ *Raw Sienna + Warm White + 　　Yellow Oxide 2:2:1
☐ Potter's Clay 　　S: Apache H: Creamy Beige
☐ *WN Yellow Ochre + White + Alizarin Crimson 　　+Ultramarine Blue 4:3:1:1

NOTES

T C S # BR-1-2-4

AMERICANA	☐ Honey Brown 　　S: Milk Chocolate H: Golden Straw
CERAMCOAT	☐ Golden Brown 　　S: Raw Sienna H: Straw
FOLK ART	☐ English Mustard 　　S: Burnt Sienna H: Lemonade
JO SONJA	☐ Raw Sienna
1837 LEGACY	☐ *Brown Sugar + Yellow Oxide 2:1
OIL EQUIV.	☐ ARC Raw Sienna, 　　REM Raw Sienna

NOTES

T C S # BR-1-2-5

☐ Raw Sienna 　　S: Burnt Umber H: Honey Brown
☐ Raw Sienna 　　S: Brown Iron Oxide H: Antique Gold
☐ * Yellow Light + Terra Cotta 2:1
☐ *Raw Sienna + Gold Oxide (T)
☐ Raw Sienna 　　S: Nutmeg H: Sweet Cream
☐ WN Raw Sienna

NOTES

TCS # BR-1-2-7

AMERICANA	☐ Terra Cotta S: Burnt Sienna H: Pumpkin
CERAMCOAT	☐ *Raw Sienna + Toffee Brown 3:1
FOLK ART	☐ Buckskin Brown S: Dark Brown H: Linen
JO SONJA	☐ *Raw Sienna + Burnt Sienna 3:1
1837 LEGACY	☐ *Raw Sienna + Warm Brown 3:1
OIL EQUIV.	☐ PRI Raw Sienna

NOTES

TCS # BR-1-3-5

	☐ *Raw Sienna + Honey Brown 4:1
	☐ *Raw Sienna + Golden Brown 4:1
	☐ *English Mustard + Buckskin Brown 4:1
	☐ *Raw Sienna + Yellow Oxide 4:1
	☐ Brown Sugar S: Warm Brown H: Oak
	☐ *WN Raw Sienna + White + GRUM Burnt Sienna 8:1:1

NOTES

TCS # BR-2-2-2

AMERICANA	☐ French Vanilla S: Yellow Ochre H: Buttermilk
CERAMCOAT	☐ Flesh Tan S: Spice Tan H: Light Ivory
FOLK ART	☐ French Vanilla S: Teddy Bear Tan H: White
JO SONJA	☐ *Warm White + Yellow Oxide 8:1
1837 LEGACY	☐ Creamy Beige S: Golden Gourd H: Sweet Cream
OIL EQUIV.	☐ ARC Naples Yellow Hue

NOTES

TCS # BR-2-2-3

	☐ *Sand + Yellow Ochre 1:1
	☐ AC Flesh S: Spice Tan H: Antique White
	☐ Almond Parfait S: Acorn Brown H: Georgia Peach
	☐ *Opal + Provincial Beige 6:1
	☐ Warm Beige S: Tundra H: Sweet Cream
	☐ *WN Raw Sienna + White + Bright Red + Cadmium Yellow Pale 3:4:1:1

NOTES

TCS # BR-2-2-4

AMERICANA	☐ *Antique Gold + Sable Brown 3:1
CERAMCOAT	☐ Spice Tan S: Spice Brown H: Flesh Tan
FOLK ART	☐ Honeycomb S: Coffee Bean H: Linen
JO SONJA	☐ *Raw Sienna + Yellow Oxide + Warm White 2:1:1
1837 LEGACY	☐ Cappuccino S: Warm Brown H: Golden Rod
OIL EQUIV.	☐ *WN Cad. Yellow Pale + White + Alizarin Crimson + French Ultramarine 4:3:1:1

NOTES

TCS # BR-2-2-5

	☐ *Raw Sienna + Antique Gold 1:1
	☐ Mocha Brown S: Brown Iron Oxide H: Maple Sugar Tan
	☐ Raw Sienna (AP) S: Nutmeg H: French Vanilla
	☐ *Yellow Oxide + Burnt Sienna 4:1
	☐ Mocha S: Warm Brown H: Corn Silk
	☐ *WN R. Sienna + White + Alizarin Crimson + French Ultramarine 4:2:1:1

NOTES

TCS # BR-2-2-6

AMERICANA	☐ Light Cinnamon S: Burnt Umber H: Sable Brown
CERAMCOAT	☐ Autumn Brown S: Brown Iron Oxide H: Light Chocolate
FOLK ART	☐ *Nutmeg + Maple Syrup 1:1
JO SONJA	☐ *Raw Sienna + Indian Red Oxide 4:1
1837 LEGACY	☐ Nutmeg S: Dark Brown H: Raw Sienna
OIL EQUIV.	☐ *WN Burnt Sienna + Burnt Umber + Bright Red + White 1:1:1:8

NOTES

TCS # BR-2-2-7

AMERICANA	☐ Milk Chocolate S: Burnt Umber H: Sable Brown
CERAMCOAT	☐ Spice Brown S: Burnt Umber H: Light Chocolate
FOLK ART	☐ Nutmeg S: Burnt Umber H: Country Twill
JO SONJA	☐ *Raw Sienna + Indian Red Oxide 6:1
1837 LEGACY	☐ Warm Brown S: Chestnut H: Devon Cream
OIL EQUIV.	☐ *WN Burnt Sienna + Burnt Umber + White 2:1:2

NOTES

TCS # BR-2-2-8

AMERICANA	☐ *Light Cinnamon + Dark Chocolate (T)
CERAMCOAT	☐ Dark Brown S: Dark Chocolate H: Toffee Brown
FOLK ART	☐ *Chocolate Fudge + Coffee Bean (T)
JO SONJA	☐ *Raw Umber + Brown Earth 1:1
1837 LEGACY	☐ Dark Brown Sugar S: Espresso H: Hazelnut
OIL EQUIV.	☐ REM Stil De Grain Brun

NOTES

TCS # BR-2-3-3

AMERICANA	☐ *Yellow Ochre + Terra Cotta 1:1
CERAMCOAT	☐ *Maple Sugar Tan + Spice Tan 1:1
FOLK ART	☐ Cappuccino S: Buckskin Brown H: Buttercrunch
JO SONJA	☐ *Opal + Raw Sienna 2:1
1837 LEGACY	☐ *Chamois + Cappuccino 1:1
OIL EQUIV.	☐ *WN White + Raw Sienna + Bright Red + Cadmium Yellow Pale 3:4:1:1

NOTES

TCS # BR-2-4-4

AMERICANA	☐ *Yellow Ochre + Burnt Umber (T)
CERAMCOAT	☐ *Sandstone + Palomino Tan 2:1
FOLK ART	☐ Camel S: Honeycomb H: Clay Bisque
JO SONJA	☐ *Provincial Beige + Yellow Oxide 5:1
1837 LEGACY	☐ Golden Gourd S: Apache H: Oatmeal
OIL EQUIV.	☐ *WN White + Raw Sienna + French Ultramarine 10:6:1

NOTES

TCS # BR-2-4-6

AMERICANA	☐ *Antique Gold + Antique Gold Deep 2:1
CERAMCOAT	☐ Cloudberry Tan S: Boston Fern H: Maple Sugar Tan
FOLK ART	☐ *Teddy Bear Tan + Yellow Ochre 3:1
JO SONJA	☐ *Yellow Light + Fawn 1:1
1837 LEGACY	☐ Apache S: Olivette H: Oak
OIL EQUIV.	☐ *WN Yellow Ochre + Olive Green 3:1

NOTES

BRAND **COLOR** **COLOR**

TCS #BR-2-5-4

AMERICANA	☐ *Antique Gold + Antique Gold Deep 2:1
CERAMCOAT	☐ *Golden Brown + Mustard 1:1
FOLK ART	☐ *Harvest Gold + Teddy Bear Tan 1:1
JO SONJA	☐ *Yellow Oxide + Turner's Yellow 2:1
1837 LEGACY	☐ Oak S: Raw Sienna H: Caribou
OIL EQUIV.	☐ *WN Gold Ochre + Naples Yellow 2:1

NOTES

TCS # BR-2-5-8

AMERICANA	☐ *Antique Gold Deep + Antique Green 5:1
CERAMCOAT	☐ *Cloudberry Tan + Raw Sienna 4:1
FOLK ART	☐ *Teddy Bear Tan + English Mustard 1:1
JO SONJA	☐ *Raw Sienna + Yellow Oxide + Warm White 4:1:1
1837 LEGACY	☐ *Apache + Raw Sienna + Olive Branch 4:1:T
OIL EQUIV.	☐ PRI Yellow Ochre, REM Yellow Ochre, WN Gold Ochre

NOTES

TCS #BR-4-4-4

AMERICANA	☐ *Sable Brown + White (T)
CERAMCOAT	☐ Territorial Beige S: Burnt Umber H: Trail
FOLK ART	☐ *Honeycomb + Coffee Bean (T)
JO SONJA	☐ Provincial Beige
1837 LEGACY	☐ Tundra S: Brown Iron Oxide H: Devon Cream
OIL EQUIV.	☐ *WN White + Burnt Umber + Raw Sienna 2:1:1

NOTES

TCS # BR-4-4-5

AMERICANA	☐ Sable Brown S: Burnt Umber H: Mink Tan
CERAMCOAT	☐ *Spice Brown + White 2:1
FOLK ART	☐ *Teddy Bear Tan + Teddy Bear Brown 1:1
JO SONJA	☐ *Raw Sienna + Opal 3:1
1837 LEGACY	☐ *Warm Brown + Chamois 2:1
OIL EQUIV.	☐ *WN White + REM Transparent Oxide Brown + WN Olive Green 3:2:T

NOTES

TCS #BR-5-1-5

AMERICANA	☐ *Light Cinnamon + Dark Chocolate 4:1
CERAMCOAT	☐ Brown Iron Oxide S: Walnut H: Toffee Brown
FOLK ART	☐ Maple Syrup S: Burnt Umber H: Clay Bisque
JO SONJA	☐ Brown Earth
1837 LEGACY	☐ Brown Iron Oxide S: Espresso H: Doeskin
OIL EQUIV.	☐ WN Brown Madder Alizarin

NOTES

TCS #BR-5-1-6

AMERICANA	☐ *Light Cinnamon + Dark Chocolate 1:1
CERAMCOAT	☐ Brown Velvet S: Walnut H: Toffee Brown
FOLK ART	☐ Dark Brown S: Burnt Umber H: Light Red Oxide
JO SONJA	☐ *Raw Umber + Brown Earth 1:1
1837 LEGACY	☐ Chestnut S: Espresso H: Hazelnut
OIL EQUIV.	☐ *WN Burnt Umber + Alizarin Crimson + White 5:3:2

NOTES

	T C S # BR-5-2-7
AMERICANA	☐ *Mink Tan + Sable Brown 1:1
CERAMCOAT	☐ Toffee Brown S: Brown Iron Oxide H: Light Chocolate
FOLK ART	☐ *Buckskin Brown + Country Twill 4:1
JO SONJA	☐ *Raw Sienna + Provincial Beige 4:1
1837 LEGACY	☐ *Milk Chocolate + Warm Brown 1:1
OIL EQUIV.	☐ *WN White + REM Transparent Oxide Green + WN Olive Green 6:4:1

NOTES

	T C S # BR-5-4-2
AMERICANA	☐ Toffee S: Sable Brown H: Buttermilk
	☐ *White + Bambi 2:1
	☐ *Milkshake + Acorn Brown 3:1
	☐ *White + Fawn 2:1
	☐ Flesh S: Chamois H: Creammette
	☐ *WN White + Raw Sienna + Burnt Umber 8:4:1

NOTES

	T C S # BR-5-4-3
AMERICANA	☐ Cashmere Beige S: Sable Brown H: Toffee
CERAMCOAT	☐ *Bambi + White 1:1
FOLK ART	☐ *Milkshake + Acorn Brown 2:1
JO SONJA	☐ *Fawn + White 1:1
1837 LEGACY	☐ *White + Tundra 1:1
OIL EQUIV.	☐ *REM White + Transparent Oxide Brown 4:1

NOTES

	T C S # BR-5-4-4
	☐ Mink Tan S: Light Cinnamon H: Cashmere Beige
	☐ Bambi Brown S: Brown Iron Oxide H: Dunes Beige
	☐ Mushroom S: Dark Gray H: Clay Bisque
	☐ Fawn
	☐ Doeskin S: Nutmeg H: Devon Cream
	☐ *REM White + REM Transparent Oxide Brown + WN Olive Green 3:1:T

NOTES

	T C S # BR-6-2-5
AMERICANA	☐ *Terra Cotta + Burnt Orange 1:1
CERAMCOAT	☐ Burnt Sienna S: Brown Iron Oxide H: Georgia Clay
FOLK ART	☐ *Terra Cotta + Burnt Sienna (AP) 3:1
JO SONJA	☐ *Gold Oxide + Burnt Sienna 3:1
1837 LEGACY	☐ Burnt Sienna S: Cinnabar H: Mango
OIL EQUIV.	☐ WN Burnt Sienna

NOTES

	T C S # BR-6-2-6
	☐ Burnt Sienna S: Antique Maroon H: Georgia Clay
	☐ *Brown Iron Oxide + Red Iron Oxide 1:1
	☐ Burnt Sienna (AP) S: Burnt Umber H: Clay Bisque
	☐ Burnt Sienna
	☐ *Brown Iron Oxide + Red Iron Oxide 1:1
	☐ ARC Burnt Sienna, PRI Burnt Sienna

NOTES

T C S # BR-6-2-9

AMERICANA ☐ Russet
    S: Black Plum H: Brandy Wine

CERAMCOAT ☐ *Sonoma + Burnt Umber 1:1

FOLK ART ☐ *Burnt Carmine + Burnt Umber 1:1

JO SONJA ☐ *Indian Red Oxide + Brown Earth 1:1

1837 LEGACY ☐ *Cinnabar + Dark Brown Sugar 1:1

OIL EQUIV. ☐ *WN Burnt Umber + Alizarin Crimson +
    White 4:3:1

NOTES

T C S # BR-6-4-2

☐ Mocha (D)
    S: Light Cinnamon H: Mocha + White 1:1
☐ Dunes Beige
    S: Dark Flesh H: Santa's Flesh
☐ *Almond Parfait + Acorn Brown 2:1

☐ *Smoked Pearl + Gold Oxide +
    Raw Sienna 10:1:1
☐ Toast
    S: Apricot H: Corn Silk
☐ *WN White + Raw Sienna + Cadmium Red
    Light 10:4:1

NOTES

T C S # BR-6-4-3

AMERICANA ☐ Mocha
    S: Light Cinnamon H: Mocha + White 1:1

CERAMCOAT ☐ Light Chocolate (D)
    S: Brown Iron Oxide H: A.C. Flesh

FOLK ART ☐ *Almond Parfait + Acorn Brown 1:1

JO SONJA ☐ *Opal + Warm White + Gold Oxide 3:1:1

1837 LEGACY ☐ *Milk Chocolate + White 1:1

OIL EQUIV. ☐ *WN White + GRUM Burnt Sienna 8:1

NOTES

T C S # BR-6-4-4

☐ *Mocha + Terra Cotta (T)

☐ Light Chocolate
    S: Brown Iron Oxide H: A.C. Flesh
☐ *Acorn Brown + Almond Parfait 2:1

☐ *Warm White + Gold Oxide + Raw Sienna 9:1:1

☐ Milk Chocolate
    S: Warm Brown H: Devon Cream
☐ *REM White + Transparent Oxide Brown 3:1

NOTES

T C S # BR-6-4-5

AMERICANA ☐ *Shading Flesh + Terra Cotta 1:1

CERAMCOAT ☐ *Toffee Brown + Burnt Sienna (T)

FOLK ART ☐ Acorn Brown
    S: Coffee Bean H: Almond Parfait

JO SONJA ☐ *Fawn + Burnt Sienna 4:1

1837 LEGACY ☐ Hazelnut
    S: Warm Brown H: Devon Cream

OIL EQUIV. ☐ *WN White + Burnt Sienna + Burnt Umber +
    Bright Red + Raw Sienna 20:1:1:1:1

NOTES

T C S # BR-6-4-7

☐ *Light Cinnamon + Mink Tan 4:1

☐ *Burnt Umber + Territorial Beige 1:1

☐ Teddy Bear Brown
    S: Burnt Umber H: Clay Bisque
☐ *Brown Earth + Provincial Beige 1:1

☐ *Dark Brown Sugar + Tundra 1:1

☐ *WN Burnt Sienna + White + Burnt Umber +
    Bright Red 4:2:2:1

NOTES

T C S # BR-7-4-3

AMERICANA   ☐ *Antique White + Mississippi Mud (T)

CERAMCOAT   ☐ Trail Tan
      S: Territorial Beige   H: Putty

FOLK ART   ☐ Country Twill
      S: Teddy Bear Brown   H: Linen

JO SONJA   ☐ *Smoked Pearl + Provincial Beige 1:1

1837 LEGACY   ☐ Taupe
      S: Sterling Grey   H: Antique Lace

OIL EQUIV.   ☐ *WN Burnt Umber + White +
      French Ultramarine + Raw Sienna 3:10:1:2

NOTES

T C S # BR-7-5-7

☐ *Light Cinnamon + Burnt Umber 1:1

☐ *Burnt Umber + Territorial Beige 1:1

☐ Coffee Bean
   S: Burnt Umber   H: Country Twill

☐ *Raw Umber + Brown Earth +
   Provincial Beige 6:6:1

☐ *Burnt Umber + Tundra 1:1

☐ *WN Burnt Umber + White + Bright Red 4:4:1

NOTES

T C S # BR-7-5-8

AMERICANA   ☐ Asphaltum
      S: Soft Black   H: Light Cinnamon

CERAMCOAT   ☐ Burnt Umber
      S: Black   H: Light Chocolate

FOLK ART   ☐ *Burnt Sienna + Burnt Umber (AP) 1:1

JO SONJA   ☐ *Raw Umber + Brown Earth 2:1

1837 LEGACY   ☐ Burnt Umber
      S: Espresso   H: Milk Chocolate

OIL EQUIV.   ☐ REM Burnt Umber,
      WN Burnt Umber

NOTES

T C S # BR-7-6-1

☐ *White + Warm Neutral 2:1

☐ *White + Wild Rice 2:1

☐ Parchment
   S: Milkshake   H: White

☐ *Warm White + Smoked Pearl + Opal 4:1:1

☐ *White + Burnt Almond 2:1

☐ *WN White + Naples Yellow + French Ultramine
   + Alizarin Crimson 10:2:1:1

NOTES

T C S # BR-7-6-3

AMERICANA   ☐ Warm Neutral
      S: Mississippi Mud   H: White

CERAMCOAT   ☐ Wild Rice
      S: Misty Mauve   H: Santa's Flesh

FOLK ART   ☐ Milkshake
      S: Acorn Brown   H: White

JO SONJA   ☐ Opal

1837 LEGACY   ☐ Burnt Almond
      S: Dusty Rose   H: Corn Silk

OIL EQUIV.   ☐ *WN White + Cad. Yellow Pale + French
      Ultramarine + Alizarin Crimson 5:1:1:1

NOTES

T C S # BR-7-6-8

☐ Dark Chocolate
   S: Soft Black   H: Milk Chocolate

☐ *Burnt Umber + Dark Chocolate 1:1

☐ Asphaltum (AP)
   S: Pure Black   H: Raw Sienna

☐ Burnt Umber (D)

☐ *Burnt Umber + Espresso 1:1

☐ ARC Brown Earth,
   REM Transparent Oxide Red,
   *WN Burnt Umber + White 2:1

NOTES

TCS # BR-7-6-9

AMERICANA	☐ Burnt Umber S: Asphaltum H: Milk Chocolate
CERAMCOAT	☐ Dark Burnt Umber S: Black H: Light Chocolate
FOLK ART	☐ *Burnt Umber + Burnt Sienna (AP) 2:1
JO SONJA	☐ Burnt Umber
1837 LEGACY	☐ *Espresso + Raw Umber 2:1
OIL EQUIV.	☐ ARC Burnt Umber, PRI Burnt Umber, REM Trans. Oxide Brown, WN Vandyke Brown

NOTES

TCS # BR-8-5-7

AMERICANA	☐ Raw Umber S: Soft Black H: Mississippi Mud
CERAMCOAT	☐ Walnut S: Black H: Trail Tan
FOLK ART	☐ *Coffee Bean + White 3:1
JO SONJA	☐ *Raw Umber + Provincial Beige 2:1
1837 LEGACY	☐ Raw Umber S: Black H: Spider Web
OIL EQUIV.	☐ WN Raw Umber

NOTES

TCS # BR-8-6-5

AMERICANA	☐ Mississippi Mud S: Raw Umber H: Sable Brown
CERAMCOAT	☐ *Dark Chocolate + Trail 2:1
FOLK ART	☐ *Coffee Bean + White 3:1
JO SONJA	☐ *Raw Umber + Provincial Beige 1:1
1837 LEGACY	☐ *Espresso + Taupe 2:1
OIL EQUIV.	☐ *WN Burnt Umber + White 1:1

NOTES

TCS # BR-8-6-8

AMERICANA	☐ Soft Black S: Lamp (Ebony) Black H: Burnt Umber
CERAMCOAT	☐ Dark Chocolate S: Black H: Territorial Beige
FOLK ART	☐ Raw Umber (AP) S: Pure Black H: Clay Bisque
JO SONJA	☐ Raw Umber or Jo Sonja Bkg Charcoal
1837 LEGACY	☐ Espresso S: Black Angus H: Tundra
OIL EQUIV.	☐ ARC Raw Umber, REM Raw Umber

NOTES

TCS # BR-8-6-9

AMERICANA	☐ Bittersweet Chocolate S: Black H: Driftwood
CERAMCOAT	☐ *Brown Iron Oxide + Black 2:1
FOLK ART	☐ Burnt Umber (AP) S: Pure Black H: Teddy Bear Tan
JO SONJA	☐ *Brown Earth + Raw Umber + Black (Carbon) 4:1:1
1837 LEGACY	☐ *Brown Iron Oxide + Black 2:1
OIL EQUIV.	☐ PRI Van Dyke Brown, *WN Burnt Umber + French Ultramarine 6:5

NOTES

TCS # BK-1-7-8

AMERICANA	☐ Charcoal Grey S: Soft Black H: Neutral Grey
CERAMCOAT	☐ *Dark Chocolate + Hippo Grey 5:1
FOLK ART	☐ Dark Gray S: Licorice H: Barn Wood
JO SONJA	☐ *Raw Umber + Black 12:1
1837 LEGACY	☐ *Espresso + Rhino Grey 5:1
OIL EQUIV.	☐ REM Warm Grey, *WN Raw Umber + White + Burnt Umber 2:2:1

NOTES

BRAND	COLOR	COLOR

T C S # BK-3-7-4

AMERICANA	☐ Driftwood
	S: Mississippi Mud H: Cool Neutral
CERAMCOAT	☐ Lichen Grey
	S: Hammered Iron H: Sandstone
FOLK ART	☐ Barn Wood
	S: Medium Gray H: Gray Mist
JO SONJA	☐ *Smoked Pearl + Provincial Beige +
	Raw Umber 7:1:1
1837 LEGACY	☐ Sterling Grey
	S: Pewter H: Spider Web
OIL EQUIV.	☐ *WN White + French Ultramarine + Burnt
	Umber + Cadmium Lemon 12:2:3:1

NOTES

T C S # BK-3-7-5

AMERICANA	☐ Driftwood (L)
	S: Mississippi Mud H: Cool Neutral
CERAMCOAT	☐ Mudstone
	S: Hammered Iron H: Sandstone
FOLK ART	☐ Barn Wood (L)
	S: Medium Gray H: Gray Mist
JO SONJA	☐ *Smoked Pearl + Nimbus Grey +
	Raw Umber 5:1:1
1837 LEGACY	☐ Arrowhead
	S: Pewter H: Spider Web
OIL EQUIV.	☐ *WN White + Burnt Umber + Prussian Blue +
	GRUM Bt. Sienna 12:3:1:2

NOTES

T C S # BK-3-7-8

AMERICANA	☐ *Neutral Gray + Avocado (T)
CERAMCOAT	☐ Hammered Iron
	S: Black Green H: Lichen Grey
FOLK ART	☐ Dapple Gray
	S: Dark Gray H: Ice Blue
JO SONJA	☐ *Moss Green + Nimbus Grey 1:1
1837 LEGACY	☐ Pewter
	S: Black Angus H: Sterling Grey
OIL EQUIV.	☐ *WN Davy's Gray + White 5:1

NOTES

T C S # BK-4-5-5

AMERICANA	☐ *Neutral Grey Toning + Buttermilk 2:1
CERAMCOAT	☐ Cadet Grey
	S: Hippo Grey H: Soft Grey
FOLK ART	☐ *Light Gray + Dapple Gray 5:1
JO SONJA	☐ Nimbus Grey or
	Jo Sonja Bkg Dove Grey
1837 LEGACY	☐ Silver Fox
	S: Rhino Grey H: Antique Lace
OIL EQUIV.	☐ *WN White + Burnt Umber + Ultra. Blue 8:2:1

NOTES

T C S # BK-5-1-2

AMERICANA	☐ Dove Grey
	S: Slate Grey H: White
CERAMCOAT	☐ *White + Black 15:1
FOLK ART	☐ Light Gray
	S: Medium Gray H: White
JO SONJA	☐ *White + Carbon Black 15:1
1837 LEGACY	☐ *White + Black 10:1
OIL EQUIV.	☐ *WN Davy's Gray + White 10:1

NOTES

T C S # BK-5-1-8

AMERICANA	☐ Black (Ebony/Lamp) (D)
	S: None H: Neutral Grey
CERAMCOAT	☐ Black (D)
	S: None H: Bridgeport Grey
FOLK ART	☐ Black, Pure (AP)
	S: None H: Medium Gray
JO SONJA	☐ Black (Carbon) (D)
1837 LEGACY	☐ Black
	S: None H: Dove Grey
OIL EQUIV.	☐ PRI Black (Ivory),
	REM Black (Ivory),
	WN Black (Ivory)

NOTES

	COLOR	COLOR

TCS #BK-5-1-9

AMERICANA	☐ Black (Ebony/Lamp) S: None H: Neutral Grey
CERAMCOAT	☐ Black S: None H: Bridgeport Gray
FOLK ART	☐ Licorice S: None H: Any lighter color
JO SONJA	☐ Black (Carbon)
1837 LEGACY	☐ Black Angus S: None H: Phantom Blue
OIL EQUIV.	☐ ARC Black (Mars), WN Black (Lamp)

NOTES

TCS #BK-5-5-1

☐ *White + Neutral Gray 12:1

☐ *White + Cadet Gray 10:1

☐ Gray Mist
S: Barn Wood H: White
☐ *White + Nimbus Grey 12:1

☐ *White + Sterling Grey 10:1

☐ *WN White + Fr. Ultramarine + Burnt Umber + Cadmium Lemon 50:2:3:1

NOTES

TCS #BK-5-5-3

AMERICANA	☐ *Dove Gray + Neutral Grey (T)
CERAMCOAT	☐ Quaker Grey S: Charcoal H: White
FOLK ART	☐ *Light Gray + Ice Blue 1:1
JO SONJA	☐ *Nimbus Grey + White 1:1
1837 LEGACY	☐ Storm Cloud S: Rhino Grey H: Dove Grey
OIL EQUIV.	☐ PRI Prima Gray

NOTES

TCS #BK-5-5-5

☐ Neutral Grey
S: Graphite H: Slate Grey
☐ Hippo Grey
S: Charcoal H: Cadet Gray
☐ Medium Gray
S: Dark Gray H: Light Gray
☐ *Black + White 1:1

☐ Rhino Grey
S: Black H: Storm Cloud
☐ *WN White + French Ultramarine + Burnt Umber 4:2:3

NOTES

TCS #BK-5-6-4

AMERICANA	☐ *Neutral Grey + Driftwood 1:1
CERAMCOAT	☐ *Quaker Grey + Lichen Grey 1:1
FOLK ART	☐ *Dapple Gray + Barn Wood 1:1
JO SONJA	☐ *Nimbus Grey + Smoked Pearl 2:1 or Jo Sonja Bkg Oakmoss
1837 LEGACY	☐ *Pioneer Grey + Pewter 2:1
OIL EQUIV.	☐ *WN White + Burnt Umber + Ultra. Blue + Winsor Yellow 10:4:3:1

NOTES

TCS #BK-6-2-1

☐ *White + Dove Grey + Grey Sky 4:4:1

☐ Soft Grey
S: Drizzle Grey H: Magnolia White
☐ *Gray Mist + Dove Gray 4:1

☐ *White + Nimbus Grey + Payne's Grey 16:1:1

☐ *White + Pioneer Grey 15:1

☐ *REM White + Warm Grey 6:1

NOTES

T C S # BK-6-2-2

AMERICANA	☐ *Dove Grey + Grey Sky 4:1
CERAMCOAT	☐ Drizzle Grey S: Bridgeport Grey H: White
FOLK ART	☐ *Light Gray + Porcelain Blue 12:1
JO SONJA	☐ *White + Nimbus Grey + Payne's Grey 12:1:1
1837 LEGACY	☐ Pelican S: Pioneer Grey H: White
OIL EQUIV.	☐ *WN White + Ivory Black 2:1

NOTES

T C S # BK-6-2-8

☐ *Slate Grey + Black 1:1
☐ Storm Grey S: Black H: Rain Grey
☐ Charcoal Gray S: Licorice H: Dark Gray
☐ *Nimbus Grey + White + Payne's Grey 10:1:1
☐ Soft Kohl (D) S: Black Angus H: Dove Grey
☐ ARC Warm Grey

NOTES

T C S # BK-6-2-9

AMERICANA	☐ Graphite S: Lamp (Ebony) Black H: Neutral Grey
CERAMCOAT	☐ Charcoal S: None H: Bridgeport Grey
FOLK ART	☐ *Charcoal Gray + Black 4:1
JO SONJA	☐ *Black + Payne's Grey + White 4:4:1
1837 LEGACY	☐ Soft Kohl S: Black Angus H: Dove Grey
OIL EQUIV.	☐ WN Charcoal Grey

NOTES

T C S # BK-7-2-3

☐ Slate Grey S: Deep Midnight Blue H: Grey Sky
☐ Bridgeport Grey S: Charcoal H: Drizzle Grey
☐ *Whipped Berry + Payne's Gray (T)
☐ *Nimbus Grey + French Blue 12:1
☐ Dove Grey S: French Blue Grey H: Pelican
☐ *REM White + Warm Grey + WN French Ultramarine 4:3:1

NOTES

T C S # BK-7-2-4

AMERICANA	☐ Slate Grey (L) S: Deep Midnight Blue H: Grey Sky
CERAMCOAT	☐ Rain Grey S: Fjord Blue H: Bridgeport Grey
FOLK ART	☐ *Porcelain Blue + Black 3:1
JO SONJA	☐ *Nimbus Grey + French Blue 6:1
1837 LEGACY	☐ *Slate Blue + White 1:1
OIL EQUIV.	☐ *WN Ivory Black + White 4:1

NOTES

T C S # BK-8-2-3

☐ Grey Sky S: Slate Grey H: White
☐ *Drizzle Grey + Blue Jay (T)
☐ Dove Gray S: Charcoal Gray H: White
☐ *Nimbus Grey + White + Sapphire 1:1:T
☐ *Pelican + Blue Birds (T)
☐ *WN White + French Ultramarine + Burnt Umber + Cadmium Yellow 30:4:2:1

NOTES

T C S # WH-3-7-5

AMERICANA	☐ Cool Neutral S: Mississippi Mud H: White
CERAMCOAT	☐ *Sandstone + Lichen Grey 5:1
FOLK ART	☐ *Clay Bisque + Barn Wood (T)
JO SONJA	☐ *Smoked Pearl + Nimbus Grey 12:1
1837 LEGACY	☐ *Spider Web + Sterling Grey 5:1
OIL EQUIV.	☐ *WN White + Raw Sienna + GRUM Greenish Umber 40:10:1

NOTES

T C S # WH-3-7-7

AMERICANA	☐ *French Vanilla + Driftwood 1:1
CERAMCOAT	☐ *Flesh Tan + Lichen Grey 1:1
FOLK ART	☐ *Barn Wood + Clay Bisque 1:1
JO SONJA	☐ *Smoked Pearl + Raw Sienna + Nimbus Grey 2:1:1 or Jo Sonja Bkg Vellum
1837 LEGACY	☐ *Oatmeal + Pewter 3:1
OIL EQUIV.	☐ *WN White + Raw Sienna + GRUM Greenish Umber 20:10:1

NOTES

T C S # WH-5-1-1

AMERICANA	☐ White (Snow or Titanium) S: Grey Sky H: None
CERAMCOAT	☐ White S: Highlight hue of Predominant Color H: None
FOLK ART	☐ White (Titanium) (AP) S: Highlight hue of predominant color H: None
JO SONJA	☐ White (Titanium)
1837 LEGACY	☐ White S: Highlight hue of predominant color H: None
OIL EQUIV.	☐ ARC White (Titanium), REM White (Titanium), WN White (Titanium)

NOTES

T C S # WH-5-1-2

AMERICANA	☐ White Wash S: Grey Sky H: None
CERAMCOAT	☐ Magnolia White S: Highlight Hue of Predominant Color H: None
FOLK ART	☐ Wicker White S: Any darker color H: None
JO SONJA	☐ Titanium White (L)
1837 LEGACY	☐ White (L) S: Highlight of Predominant Hue H: None
OIL EQUIV.	☐ ARC White (Soft Formula Titanium), PRI White (Titanium)

NOTES

T C S # WH-6-3-2

AMERICANA	☐ *Eggshell + White 1:1
CERAMCOAT	☐ *White + Lichen Grey (T)
FOLK ART	☐ Tapioca S: Butter Pecan H: White
JO SONJA	☐ *White + Smoked Pearl 5:1
1837 LEGACY	☐ *White + Sterling Grey (T)
OIL EQUIV.	☐ *WN White + Raw Sienna + French Ultramarine 20:6:1

NOTES

T C S # WH-6-3-4

AMERICANA	☐ Eggshell S: Shale Green H: Light Buttermilk
CERAMCOAT	☐ *White + Lichen Grey 6:1
FOLK ART	☐ *Tapioca + Barn Wood 2:1
JO SONJA	☐ *White + Smoked Pearl + Nimbus Grey 3:1:T
1837 LEGACY	☐ *White + Pewter Grey 6:1
OIL EQUIV.	☐ *WN White + Olive Green 3:1

NOTES

T C S # WH-6-4-1

AMERICANA	☐ *White + Warm Neutral 18:1
CERAMCOAT	☐ Oyster White S: Santa's Flesh H: White
FOLK ART	☐ *White + Milkshake 15:1
JO SONJA	☐ *White + Opal 15:1
1837 LEGACY	☐ *White + Antique Lace 1:1
OIL EQUIV.	☐ *WN White + Raw Sienna 12:1

NOTES

T C S # WH-6-4-2

☐ *White + Eggshell 4:1
☐ *White + Oyster White 1:1
☐ *Tapioca + Gray Mist 1:1
☐ *White + Opal + Nimbus Grey 12:1:1
☐ Antique Lace S: Spider Web H: White
☐ *WN White + Yellow Ochre + GRUM Greenish Umber 20:3:1

NOTES

T C S # WH-6-4-5

AMERICANA	☐ Desert Sand (D) S: Khaki Tan H: Sand
CERAMCOAT	☐ Raw Linen S: Lichen Grey H: White
FOLK ART	☐ Clay Bisque (D) S: Coffee Bean H: White
JO SONJA	☐ Smoked Pearl (D)
1837 LEGACY	☐ *Spider Web + White 2:1
OIL EQUIV.	☐ *White + Raw Umber + Cadmium Lemon 12:3:1

NOTES

T C S # WH-6-4-6

☐ Desert Sand S: Khaki Tan H: Sand
☐ Sandstone S: Lichen Grey H: Antique White
☐ Clay Bisque S: Coffee Bean H: White
☐ Smoked Pearl
☐ Spider Web S: Arrowhead H: Antique Lace
☐ *WN White + Burnt Umber + Fr. Ultramarine 30:2:1

NOTES

T C S # WH-6-4-9

AMERICANA	☐ Khaki Tan S: Mississippi Mud H: Desert Sand
CERAMCOAT	☐ *Trail + Sandstone 1:1
FOLK ART	☐ Butter Pecan S: Maple Syrup H: White
JO SONJA	☐ *Smoked Pearl + Prov. Beige + Raw Umber 5:1:1
1837 LEGACY	☐ *Taupe + Spider Web 1:1
OIL EQUIV.	☐ *WN Burnt Umber + White + French Ultramarine + Raw Sienna 3:6:1:1

NOTES

T C S # WH-7-3-4

☐ Antique White S: Mink Tan H: Sand
☐ *Trail + White 1:1
☐ Linen S: Nutmeg H: White
☐ *Smoked Pearl + Provincial Beige 1:1
☐ *Taupe + White 1:1
☐ *WN White + Burnt Umber + Raw Sienna + French Ultramarine 25:3:2:1

NOTES

T C S # WH-8-2-1

AMERICANA	☐ *Light Buttermilk + White 1:1
CERAMCOAT	☐ *Light Ivory + White 1:1
FOLK ART	☐ Ivory White S: Taffy H: White
JO SONJA	☐ *Warm White + White 1:1
1837 LEGACY	☐ *Birch White + White 1:1
OIL EQUIV.	☐ *WN White + Cadmium Yellow Pale 30:1

NOTES

T C S # WH-8-2-2

☐ Light Buttermilk
  S: Desert Sand H: White
☐ Light Ivory
  S: Ivory H: White
☐ Warm White (AP)
  S: Clay Bisque H: White
☐ Warm White or
  Jo Sonja Bkg Soft White
☐ Birch White
  S: Devon Cream H: White
☐ ARC Zinc White,
  *WN White + Naples Yellow 20:1

NOTES

T C S # WH-8-2-3

AMERICANA	☐ *Light Buttermilk + Buttermilk 1:1
CERAMCOAT	☐ Butter Cream S: Flesh Tan H: White
FOLK ART	☐ *Warm White + Taffy 1:1
JO SONJA	☐ Warm White (L)
1837 LEGACY	☐ Creamette S: Flesh H: White
OIL EQUIV.	☐ *WN White + Naples Yellow 4:1

NOTES

T C S # WH-8-2-4

☐ Buttermilk
  S: Yellow Ochre H: White
☐ Antique White
  S: Ivory H: White
☐ *Taffy + White 2:1

☐ *Warm White + Turner's Yellow (T)

☐ Sweet Cream
  S: Oatmeal H: White
☐ *WN White + Cadmium Yellow Pale 20:1

NOTES

T C S # WH-8-2-6

AMERICANA	☐ Sand S: Yellow Ochre H: Light Buttermilk
CERAMCOAT	☐ Ivory S: Old Parchment H: Light Ivory
FOLK ART	☐ Taffy S: Camel H: Tapioca
JO SONJA	☐ *Warm White + Turner's Yellow 12:1
1837 LEGACY	☐ Devon Cream S: Corn Silk H: White
OIL EQUIV.	☐ *WN White + Cad. Yellow Pale + Ultramarine Blue + Alizarin Crimson 10:2:1:1

NOTES

T C S # WH-8-2-8

☐ *Antique White + Raw Sienna (T)

☐ *Sandstone + Trail (T)

☐ *Camel + White 1:1

☐ *Smoked Pearl + Raw Sienna (T)

☐ Oatmeal
  S: Creamy Beige H: Creamette
☐ *WN White + Yellow Ochre + Raw Sienna +
  GRUM Greenish Umber 20:3:2:1

NOTES

Alphabetic Index

Choose a color name from the alphabetic index. This index lists the color names in brand order. Select the brand of paint listed in your project. The index will list the TCS# and the page number.

Americana™ by DecoArt

Color Name	Pg#	TCS#
Admiral Blue	49	BV-9-6-8
Alizarin Crimson	37	RE-6-4-5
Antique Gold	19	YE-6-4-5
Antique Gold Deep	76	YG-9-4-6
Antique Green	75	YG-8-8-7
Antique Maroon	34	RE-5-5-8
Antique Mauve	38	RE-6-5-7
Antique Rose	29	RO-8-3-7
Antique Teal	62	BG-5-3-8
Antique White	89	WH-7-3-4
Arbor Green	68	GR-3-7-5
Asphaltum	83	BR-7-5-8
Avocado	73	YG-4-3-6
Baby Blue	52	BL-5-2-2
Baby Pink	36	RE-6-3-2
Base Flesh	25	OR-6-7-2
Berry Red	35	RE-6-1-6
Bittersweet Chocolate	84	BR-8-6-9
Black (Ebony/Lamp)	86	BK-5-1-9
Black Forest Green	67	GR-3-5-8
Black Green	69	GR-5-3-9
Black Plum	40	RE-7-2-9
Blue Chiffon	55	BL-6-1-2
Blue Green	61	BG-4-1-8
Blue Haze	59	BG-2-4-9
Blue Mist	58	BG-1-7-2
Blue Violet	49	BV-9-1-8
Blue/Grey Mist	51	BL-4-9-5
Blueberry	57	BL-7-4-9
Bluegrass Green	62	BG-5-1-6
Blush Flesh	30	RE-3-2-6
Boysenberry Pink	40	RV-1-2-5
Brandy Wine	33	RE-4-6-8
Bright Green	71	GR-8-2-4
Brilliant Red	31	RE-4-1-6
Burgundy Wine	37	RE-6-4-8
Burnt Orange	28	RO-5-4-5
Burnt Sienna	81	BR-6-2-6
Burnt Umber	84	BR-7-6-9
Buttermilk	90	WH-8-2-4
Cadmium Orange	26	RO-5-1-7
Cadmium Red	31	RE-4-1-5
Cadmium Yellow	17	YE-5-1-6
Calico Red	34	RE-5-1-4
Camel	77	BR-1-2-2
Cashmere Beige	81	BR-5-4-3
Celery Green	71	GR-7-9-4
Charcoal Grey	84	BK-1-7-8
Cherry Red	34	RE-5-1-6
Colonial Green	58	BG-1-7-4
Cool Neutral	88	WH-3-7-5
Coral Rose	29	RO-8-3-4
Country Blue	48	BV-8-3-4
Country Red	31	RE-4-2-5
Cranberry Wine	38	RE-6-5-8
Crimson Tide	31	RE-4-2-7
Dark Chocolate	83	BR-7-6-8
Dark Pine	67	GR-3-3-6
Deep Burgundy	37	RE-6-4-9
Deep Midnight Blue	53	BL-5-2-8
Deep Periwinkle	47	BV-5-3-6
Deep Teal	65	BG-9-6-9
DeLane's Cheek Color	29	RO-8-3-6
DeLane's Dark Flesh	23	OR-5-9-8
DeLane's Deep Shadow	28	RO-5-4-6
Desert Sand	89	WH-6-4-6
Desert Turquoise	61	BG-4-4-5
Dioxazine Purple	45	VI-5-1-7
Dove Grey	85	BK-5-1-2
Dried Basil Green	75	YG-8-8-3
Driftwood	85	BK-3-7-4
Dusty Rose	25	OR-6-7-3
Eggshell	88	WH-6-3-4
Evergreen	73	YG-4-3-7
Flesh Tone	24	OR-6-3-4
Forest Green	70	GR-6-6-6
French Grey/Blue	54	BL-5-7-4
French Mauve	39	RE-6-7-4
French Mocha	35	RE-5-8-5
French Vanilla	78	BR-2-2-2
Georgia Clay	28	RO-7-4-7
Gingerbread	28	RO-5-5-6
Golden Straw	18	YE-5-5-5
Gooseberry Pink	30	RE-3-5-5
Graphite	87	BK-6-2-9
Green Mist	68	GR-3-7-4
Grey Sky	87	BK-8-2-3
Hauser Dark Green	67	GR-3-6-8
Hauser Light Green	73	YG-4-3-3
Hauser Medium Green	70	GR-7-4-5
Heritage Brick	33	RE-4-6-7
Hi-Lite Flesh	31	RE-4-3-1
Holly Green	66	GR-3-3-5
Honey Brown	77	BR-1-2-4
Ice Blue	51	BL-4-9-2
Indian Turquoise	60	BG-3-4-3
Jade Green	69	GR-5-6-4
Kelly Green	66	GR-3-2-4
Khaki Tan	89	WH-6-4-9
Lavender	45	VI-5-1-5
Leaf Green	69	GR-5-4-7
Lemon Yellow	16	YE-4-1-4
Light Avocado	74	YG-5-6-5
Light Buttermilk	90	WH-8-2-2
Light Cinnamon	79	BR-2-2-6
Light French Blue	51	BL-4-8-4
Lilac	45	VI-5-1-2
Limeade	74	YG-7-3-2
Marigold	18	YE-6-2-6
Mauve	39	RE-6-7-5
Medium Flesh	24	OR-6-3-5
Midnite Blue	56	BL-7-2-8
Midnite Green	69	GR-5-3-8
Milk Chocolate	79	BR-2-2-7
Mink Tan	81	BR-5-4-4
Mint Julep Green	66	GR-3-3-3
Mississippi Mud	84	BR-8-6-5
Mistletoe	70	GR-6-4-5

A WORD ABOUT OUR MATCHES

A color match to exact or very close colors are listed whenever possible. When there is not an exact match, we offer mixing recipe including ratios for attaining the color. Although pigments may vary between brands, and colors can change a bit in different dye lots, we make every effort to give you an exact match.

Color Name	Pg#	TCS#
Mocha	82	BR-6-4-3
Moon Yellow	19	YE-7-7-3
Napa Red	41	RV-1-2-8
Napthol Red	34	RE-5-1-5
Navy Blue	56	BL-7-2-9
Neutral Grey	86	BK-5-5-5
Olde Gold	16	YE-2-4-5
Olive Green	74	YG-5-6-2
Orchid	42	RV-5-2-3
Oxblood	28	RO-5-4-7
Pansy Lavender	44	RV-9-2-8
Payne's Grey	53	BL-5-2-9
Peach Sherbet	27	RO-5-3-4
Peaches 'n Cream	26	RO-3-3-3
Peony Pink	36	RE-6-4-3
Petal Pink	41	RV-2-4-2
Pineapple	16	YE-4-1-2
Pink Chiffon	37	RE-6-5-1
Plantation Pine	73	YG-4-3-9
Plum	43	RV-5-8-9
Primary Blue	52	BL-5-1-5
Primary Red	36	RE-6-2-6
Primary Yellow	17	YE-5-1-7
Prussian Blue	53	BL-5-2-7
Pumpkin	22	OR-5-1-5
Raspberry	38	RE-6-5-5
Raw Sienna	77	BR-1-2-5
Raw Umber	84	BR-8-5-7
Red Iron Oxide	33	RE-4-6-5
Red Violet	41	RV-2-2-8
Reindeer Moss Green	76	YG-9-9-2
Rookwood Red	35	RE-5-6-9
Royal Fuchsia	40	RV-1-2-6
Royal Purple	44	RV-9-2-9
Russet	82	BR-6-2-9
Sable Brown	80	BR-4-4-5
Salem Blue	57	BG-1-3-3
Sand	90	WH-8-2-6
Santa Red	36	RE-6-2-7
Sapphire	50	BL-4-2-6
Sea Aqua	63	BG-7-1-3
Shading Flesh	25	OR-6-3-8
Shale Green	71	GR-7-8-4
Silver Sage Green	65	BG-8-8-3
Slate Grey	87	BK-7-2-3
Soft Black	84	BR-8-6-8
Soft Blue	57	BL-7-4-3
Soft Peach	26	RO-3-3-2
Soft Sage	70	GR-7-7-2
Spice Pink	32	RE-4-3-5
Summer Lilac	45	RV-9-6-5
Taffy Cream	18	YE-6-2-2
Tangelo Orange	26	RO-5-1-6
Tangerine	20	YO-5-1-4
Taupe	43	RV-5-8-2
Teal Green	62	BG-5-3-7
Terra Cotta	78	BR-1-2-7
Toffee	81	BR-5-4-2
Tomato Red	31	RE-4-2-6
True Blue	52	BL-5-1-6
True Ochre	19	YE-6-4-7
True Red	35	RE-6-1-5
Ultra Blue Deep	53	BL-5-2-6
Uniform Blue	55	BL-5-7-7
Victorian Blue	57	BG-1-3-8
Violet Haze	46	VI-9-6-6
Viridian Green	65	BG-9-1-8
Warm Neutral	83	BR-7-6-3
Wedgewood Blue	57	BL-7-4-8
White (Snow or Titanium)	88	WH-5-1-1
White Wash	88	WH-5-1-2
Williamsburg Blue	54	BL-5-7-5
Winter Blue	54	BL-5-5-3
Wisteria	47	BV-5-3-3
Yellow Green	75	YG-8-2-2
Yellow Light	17	YE-5-1-5
Yellow Ochre	20	YE-7-7-6

Ceramcoat® by Delta

Color Name	Pg#	TCS#
AC Flesh	78	BR-2-2-3
Adobe Red	29	RO-8-3-7
Adriatic Blue	51	BL-4-8-8
Alpine Green	65	BG-9-6-8
Antique Gold	19	YE-6-4-5
Antique Rose	30	RE-3-5-5
Antique White	90	WH-8-2-4
Apple Green	74	YG-6-2-3
Aquamarine	59	BG-2-4-5
Autumn Brown	79	BR-2-2-6
Avalon Blue	59	BG-2-4-7
Avocado	76	YG-9-8-7
Azure Blue	59	BG-3-1-6
Bahama Purple	47	BV-5-2-4
Bambi Brown	81	BR-5-4-4
Barn Red	37	RE-6-4-9
Berry Red	39	RE-7-2-5
Bittersweet Orange	21	OR-4-1-5
Black	86	BK-5-1-9
Black Cherry	37	RE-6-4-8
Black Green	69	GR-5-3-9
Blue Danube	56	BL-6-1-3
Blue Haze	58	BG-1-7-5
Blue Heaven	52	BL-5-2-2
Blue Jay	53	BL-5-2-4
Blue Lagoon	49	BV-8-3-6
Blue Mist	55	BL-6-1-2
Blue Spruce	63	BG-5-3-9
Blue Storm	55	BL-5-7-9
Blue Velvet	52	BL-5-1-9
Blue Wisp	58	BG-1-7-2
Blueberry	57	BL-7-4-8
Bonnie Blue	54	BL-5-5-5
Boston Fern	75	YG-8-8-7
Bouquet Pink	39	RE-6-7-5
Bridgeport Grey	87	BK-7-2-3
Bright Red	34	RE-5-1-6
Bright Yellow	17	YE-5-1-5
Brown Iron Oxide	80	BR-5-1-5
Brown Velvet	80	BR-5-1-6
Burgundy Rose	33	RE-4-6-8
Burnt Sienna	81	BR-6-2-5
Burnt Umber	83	BR-7-5-8
Butter Cream	90	WH-8-2-3
Butter Yellow	17	YE-5-4-5
Cactus Green	64	BG-8-6-2
Cadet Blue	55	BL-5-7-7
Cadet Grey	85	BK-4-5-5
Calypso Orange	20	YO-6-1-3
Candy Bar Brown	34	RE-5-5-8
Cape Cod Blue	54	BL-5-7-4
Cardinal Red	35	RE-6-1-6
Caribbean Blue	61	BG-4-4-3
Caucasian Flesh	24	OR-6-3-6
Cayenne	23	OR-5-9-8
Chambray Blue	54	BL-5-7-2
Charcoal	87	BK-6-2-9
Chocolate Cherry	40	RE-7-2-9
Christmas Green	69	GR-5-4-7
Chrome Green Light	72	GR-8-6-5
Cinnamon	22	OR-4-7-9
Cloudberry Tan	79	BR-2-4-6
Colonial Blue	61	BG-4-4-5
Copen Blue	56	BL-6-1-6
Coral	29	RO-8-3-4
Cornsilk Yellow	18	YE-6-2-1
Crimson	37	RE-6-4-4
Crocus Yellow	18	YE-6-2-4
Custard	18	YE-6-2-2
Dark Brown	79	BR-2-2-8
Dark Burnt Umber	84	BR-7-6-9
Dark Chocolate	84	BR-8-6-8
Dark Flesh	25	OR-6-3-8
Dark Foliage Green	66	BG-9-7-9
Dark Forest Green	73	YG-4-3-8
Dark Goldenrod	21	OR-4-7-4
Dark Jungle Green	73	YG-4-3-7

Color	#	Code	Color	#	Code	Color	#	Code
Dark Night Blue	52	BL-4-9-9	Lichen Grey	85	BK-3-7-4	Periwinkle Blue	48	BV-8-3-4
Deep Coral	32	RE-4-3-8	Light Chocolate	82	BR-6-4-4	Persimmon	30	RE-3-2-6
Deep River Green	67	GR-3-5-8	Light Foliage Green	73	YG-4-3-3	Phthalo Blue	52	BL-5-1-5
Denim Blue	50	BL-4-5-5	Light Ivory	90	WH-8-2-2	Phthalo Green	65	BG-9-1-8
Desert Sun Orange	23	OR-5-9-6	Light Jade Green	63	BG-7-1-5	Pigskin	19	YE-6-4-8
Dolphin Grey	51	BL-4-8-4	Light Sage	65	BG-8-8-1	Pine Green	72	GR-8-6-8
Dresden Flesh	23	OR-5-7-3	Light Timberline Green	76	YG-9-9-3	Pineapple Yellow	17	YE-5-2-3
Drizzle Grey	87	BK-6-2-2	Lilac	44	RV-9-2-3	Pink Angel	27	RO-5-3-3
Dunes Beige	82	BR-6-4-2	Lilac Dusk	42	RV-3-2-4	Pink Frosting	31	RE-4-3-1
Dusty Mauve	38	RE-6-5-7	Lima Green	75	YG-8-2-2	Pink Parfait	40	RE-7-6-4
Dusty Plum	43	RV-5-8-4	Lime Green	71	GR-8-2-4	Pink Quartz	38	RE-6-5-3
Dusty Purple	43	RV-5-8-8	Lisa Pink	36	RE-6-2-4	Poppy Orange	27	RO-5-1-8
Egg Plant	42	RV-5-2-7	Luscious Lemon	16	YE-4-1-4	Pretty Pink	34	RE-5-2-5
Eggshell White	68	GR-5-1-1	Magenta	41	RV-2-2-8	Prussian Blue	56	BL-7-2-9
Emerald Green	62	BG-5-1-6	Magnolia White	88	WH-5-1-2	Pumpkin	22	OR-5-1-5
Empire Gold	18	YE-6-2-6	Mallard Green	62	BG-5-1-8	Purple	45	VI-5-1-7
English Yew Green	74	YG-5-6-7	Manganese Blue	56	BL-7-2-8	Purple Dusk	48	BV-5-4-6
Fiesta Pink	30	RE-3-2-5	Maple Sugar Tan	19	YE-7-7-4	Purple Smoke	49	BV-9-7-8
Fire Red	35	RE-6-1-5	Maroon	37	RE-6-4-7	Putty	22	OR-5-2-1
Fjord Blue	51	BL-4-9-8	Medium Flesh	24	OR-6-3-5	Quaker Grey	86	BK-5-5-3
Flesh Tan	78	BR-2-2-2	Medium Foliage Green	70	GR-7-4-5	Queen Anne's Lace	21	OR-4-2-1
Fleshtone	24	OR-6-3-4	Mello Yellow	19	YE-7-7-2	Rain Grey	87	BK-7-2-4
Forest Green	72	GR-8-6-6	Mendocino Red	41	RV-1-2-8	Rainforest Green	64	BG-8-6-4
Fruit Punch	34	RE-5-3-5	Midnight Blue	53	BL-5-2-8	Raspberry	41	RV-1-4-6
Fuchsia	40	RV-1-2-5	Misty Mauve	25	OR-6-7-4	Raw Linen	89	WH-6-4-5
G.P. Purple	45	VI-5-1-4	Mocha Brown	78	BR-2-2-5	Raw Sienna	77	BR-1-2-5
Gamal Green	73	YG-4-3-9	Moroccan Red	31	RE-4-2-7	Red Iron Oxide	33	RE-4-6-5
Georgia Clay	28	RO-5-4-4	Mudstone	85	BK-3-7-5	Rhythm 'N Blue	47	BV-5-2-6
Glacier Blue	55	BL-6-1-1	Mulberry	42	RV-2-4-8	Rose Cloud	33	RE-4-4-3
Golden Brown	77	BR-1-2-4	Mustard	16	YE-2-4-5	Rose Mist	39	RE-6-7-7
Grape	42	RV-3-2-7	Napa Wine	43	RV-5-9-8	Rose Petal Pink	37	RE-6-5-1
Green Isle	68	GR-5-1-5	Napthol Crimson	34	RE-5-1-5	Rosetta Pink	25	RO-2-3-3
Green Sea	69	GR-5-4-6	Napthol Red Light	36	RE-6-2-6	Rouge	30	RE-3-2-7
Gypsy Rose	30	RE-3-5-7	Navy Blue	53	BL-5-2-6	Royal Fuchsia	41	RV-2-4-7
Hammered Iron	85	BK-3-7-8	Nector Coral	29	RE-3-2-4	Royal Plum	43	RV-5-8-9
Heritage Blue	50	BL-3-8-8	Nightfall Blue	55	BL-5-7-8	Sachet Pink	39	RE-6-7-4
Heritage Green	64	BG-7-4-5	Normandy Rose	25	OR-6-7-3	Salem Blue	57	BG-1-3-2
Hippo Grey	86	BK-5-5-5	Norsk Blue	59	BG-1-7-8	Salem Green	61	BG-4-7-8
Hunter Green	67	GR-3-6-8	Oasis Green	64	BG-7-4-3	Sandstone	89	WH-6-4-6
Hydrangea Pink	35	RE-6-2-3	Ocean Mist Blue	58	BG-1-4-2	Santa Fe Rose	23	OR-5-9-7
Ice Storm Violet	44	RV-9-6-1	Ocean Reef Blue	56	BL-6-1-5	Santa's Flesh	24	OR-6-3-1
Indiana Rose	27	RO-5-3-2	Old Parchment	19	YE-7-7-3	Sea Grass	75	YG-7-3-3
Island Coral	22	OR-5-3-4	Olive Yellow	75	YG-8-8-4	Seashell White	35	RE-6-2-1
Ivory	90	WH-8-2-6	Opaque Blue	53	BL-5-2-5	Seminole Green	73	YG-4-3-6
Jade Green	63	BG-7-1-6	Opaque Red	34	RE-5-1-4	Silver Pine	65	BG-8-8-3
Jubilee Green	70	GR-7-2-5	Opaque Yellow	17	YE-4-1-5	Soft Grey	86	BK-6-2-1
Kelly Green	70	GR-6-4-5	Orange	26	RO-5-1-7	Sonoma Wine	35	RE-5-6-9
Laguna Blue	60	BG-4-1-5	Oyster White	89	WH-6-4-1	Spice Brown	79	BR-2-2-7
Lavender	46	VI-5-8-5	Pale Mint Green	66	GR-1-4-1	Spice Tan	78	BR-2-2-4
Lavender Lace	48	BV-7-8-3	Pale Yellow	16	YE-4-1-2	Spring Green	66	GR-3-2-4
Leaf Green	72	YG-4-2-3	Palomino Tan	77	BR-1-2-3	Stonewedge Green	71	GR-7-9-4
Leprechaun	68	GR-4-6-5	Payne's Grey	53	BL-5-2-9	Storm Grey	87	BK-6-2-8
Liberty Blue	50	BL-4-5-6	Peachy Keen	24	OR-6-3-3	Straw	18	YE-5-5-5

Color Name	Pg#	TCS#
Sunbright Yellow	16	YE-4-1-3
Sweetheart Blush	40	RV-1-2-7
Tangerine	26	RO-5-1-6
Taupe	43	RV-5-8-2
Terra Cotta	21	OR-4-7-6
Territorial Beige	80	BR-4-4-4
Tide Pool Blue	54	BL-5-7-3
Timberline	77	YG-9-9-7
Toffee Brown	81	BR-5-2-7
Tomato Spice	31	RE-4-2-6
Tompte Red	36	RE-6-2-7
Trail Tan	83	BR-7-4-3
Tropic Bay Blue	60	BG-4-1-2
Truly Teal	61	BG-4-2-8
Turquoise	60	BG-4-1-4
Ultra Blue	49	BV-9-1-8
Vibrant Green	72	YG-3-2-6
Village Green	67	GR-3-7-3
Vintage Wine	44	RV-9-2-8
Violet Ice	50	BL-3-3-2
Walnut	84	BR-8-5-7
Wedgewood Blue	54	BL-5-5-3
Wedgewood Green	69	GR-5-6-4
Western Sunset Yellow	20	YO-6-1-1
White	88	WH-5-1-1
Wild Rice	83	BR-7-6-3
Wild Rose	38	RE-6-5-5
Williamsburg Blue	54	BL-5-7-5
Wisteria	43	RV-5-8-5
Woodland Night Green	65	BG-9-6-9
Yellow	17	YE-5-1-7

Folk Art® by Plaid

Color Name	Pg#	TCS#
Acorn Brown	82	BR-6-4-5
Alizarin Crimson (AP)	37	RE-6-4-8
Almond Parfait	78	BR-2-2-3
Amish Blue	51	BL-4-8-5
Apple Spice	33	RE-4-6-7
Aqua (AP)	60	BG-4-1-5
Aspen Green	66	BG-9-7-6
Asphaltum (AP)	83	BR-7-6-8
Autumn Leaves	26	RO-5-1-6
Azure Blue	59	BG-3-1-6
Baby Blue	48	BV-8-3-3
Baby Pink	36	RE-6-3-2
Ballet Pink	38	RE-6-5-2
Barn Wood	85	BK-3-7-4
Barnyard Red	31	RE-4-2-7
Basil Green	71	GR-7-7-4
Bayberry	69	GR-5-6-4
Berries 'n Cream	39	RE-6-7-4
Berry Wine	41	RV-1-2-8
Black, Pure (AP)	85	BK-5-1-8
Blue Ink	49	BV-9-6-9
Blue Ribbon	57	BG-1-3-8
Bluebell	54	BL-5-5-5
Bluebonnet	58	BG-1-7-7
Bright Peach	26	RO-3-3-3
Bright Pink	36	RE-6-4-3
Brilliant Blue	53	BL-5-2-5
Brilliant Ultramarine (AP)	52	BL-5-1-6
Buckskin Brown	78	BR-1-2-7
Burgundy	37	RE-6-4-7
Burnt Carmine (AP)	40	RE-7-2-9
Burnt Sienna (AP)	81	BR-6-2-6
Burnt Umber (AP)	84	BR-8-6-9
Butter Pecan	89	WH-6-4-9
Buttercream	16	YE-4-1-1
Buttercrunch	19	YE-7-7-4
Buttercup	18	YE-5-5-5
Calico Red	36	RE-6-2-6
Camel	79	BR-2-4-4
Cappuccino	79	BR-2-3-3
Cardinal Red	37	RE-6-4-4
Cerulean Blue (AP)	56	BL-7-2-8
Charcoal Gray	87	BK-6-2-8
Christmas Red	34	RE-5-1-5
Cinnamon	23	OR-5-9-8
Clay Bisque	89	WH-6-4-6
Clover	73	YG-4-3-6
Coastal Blue	60	BG-3-4-5
Cobalt (AP)	56	BL-6-1-6
Coffee Bean	83	BR-7-5-7
Cotton Candy	31	RE-4-3-1
Country Twill	83	BR-7-4-3
Dapple Gray	85	BK-3-7-8
Dark Brown	80	BR-5-1-6
Dark Gray	84	BK-1-7-8
Dark Plum	46	VI-5-9-7
Denim Blue	55	BL-5-7-8
Dioxazine Purple (AP)	46	VI-5-1-9
Dove Gray	87	BK-8-2-3
Emerald Isle	64	BG-8-2-9
Engine Red	35	RE-6-1-6
English Mustard	77	BR-1-2-4
Evergreen	70	GR-6-4-5
French Blue	50	BL-3-3-5
French Vanilla	78	BR-2-2-2
Fresh Foliage	72	YG-4-3-2
Fuchsia	41	RV-2-2-8
Georgia Peach	24	OR-6-3-1
Glazed Carrots	21	OR-4-1-5
Grass Green	70	GR-7-3-5
Gray Green	71	GR-7-8-4
Gray Mist	86	BK-5-5-1
Gray Plum	46	VI-5-9-4
Green	71	GR-8-2-4
Green Forest	67	GR-3-5-8
Green Meadow	70	GR-6-6-6
Green Umber (AP)	73	YG-4-4-9
Hauser Green Dark (AP)	66	BG-9-7-9
Hauser Light Green (AP)	73	YG-4-3-3
Hauser Medium Green (AP)	70	GR-7-4-5
Heartland Blue	55	BL-5-7-7
Heather	44	RV-9-2-5
Holiday Red	37	RE-6-4-5
Honeycomb	78	BR-2-2-4
Hot Pink	40	RE-7-6-5
Huckleberry	33	RE-4-6-8
Hunter Green	67	GR-3-6-8
Ice Blue (AP)	51	BL-4-9-2
Icy White	55	BL-6-1-1
Indigo	53	BL-5-2-8
Italian Sage	68	GR-3-8-4
Ivory White	90	WH-8-2-1
Kelly Green	66	GR-3-2-4
Lavender	45	VI-5-1-5
Lavender Sachet	47	BV-2-6-1
Leaf Green	67	GR-3-5-5
Lemon Custard	16	YE-4-1-4
Lemonade	18	YE-6-2-2
Licorice	86	BK-5-1-9
Light Blue	52	BL-5-2-2
Light Fuchsia	41	RV-2-4-3
Light Gray	85	BK-5-1-2
Light Periwinkle	48	BV-8-3-4
Light Red Oxide (AP)	33	RE-4-6-5
Lime Light	76	YG-9-2-4
Lime Yellow	74	YG-7-3-2
Linen	89	WH-7-3-4
Lipstick Red	34	RE-5-1-6
Magenta	40	RV-1-2-6
Maple Syrup	80	BR-5-1-5
Maroon	38	RE-6-5-8
Medium Gray	86	BK-5-5-5
Medium Orange	22	OR-5-1-5
Medium Yellow (AP)	17	YE-4-1-5
Midnight	49	BV-9-6-8
Milkshake	83	BR-7-6-3
Mint Green	64	BG-8-6-1
Mushroom	81	BR-5-4-4
Mystic Green	68	GR-4-6-5
Napthol Crimson (AP)	36	RE-6-2-8
Navy Blue	52	BL-5-1-9
Night Sky	47	BV-5-2-8
Nutmeg	79	BR-2-2-7

Color Name	Pg#	TCS #
Old Ivy	72	GR-8-6-6
Olive Green	73	YG-4-3-7
Orange Light	22	OR-5-1-4
Orchid	42	RV-5-2-3
Parchment	83	BR-7-6-1
Pastel Green	63	BG-7-1-3
Patina	60	BG-4-1-3
Payne's Gray (AP)	52	BL-4-9-9
Peach Cobbler	22	OR-5-3-4
Peach Perfection	25	RO-2-3-3
Periwinkle	48	BV-5-4-8
Pink	40	RE-7-6-4
Plum Chiffon	43	RV-5-9-8
Plum Pudding	43	RV-5-8-9
Poetry Green	68	GR-3-7-4
Poppy Red	30	RE-3-2-6
Porcelain Blue	54	BL-5-7-3
Portrait (AP)	25	OR-6-7-2
Portrait Light	33	RE-5-1-1
Potpourri Rose	39	RE-6-7-5
Primrose	32	RE-4-3-8
Promenade	27	RO-5-3-4
Prussian Blue (AP)	53	BL-5-2-7
Pure Magenta (AP)	42	RV-3-2-8
Pure Orange (AP)	26	RO-5-1-4
Purple	45	VI-5-1-7
Purple Lilac	46	VI-5-8-5
Purple Passion	43	RV-5-8-8
Raspberry Sherbert	38	RE-6-5-5
Raspberry Wine	40	RV-1-2-7
Raw Sienna (AP)	78	BR-2-2-5
Raw Umber (AP)	84	BR-8-6-8
Red Light (AP)	26	RO-5-1-7
Red Violet	42	RV-5-2-7
Rose Chiffon	33	RE-4-4-5
Rose Garden	38	RE-6-5-7
Rose Pink	38	RE-6-5-4
Rose White	35	RE-6-2-1
Salmon	29	RO-8-3-5
Sap Green (AP)	71	GR-8-3-9
School Bus Yellow	17	YE-5-1-7
Settler's Blue	54	BL-5-7-4
Shamrock	67	GR-3-5-7
Skintone	24	OR-6-3-3
Sky Blue	58	BG-1-4-2
Slate Blue	51	BL-4-8-8
Southern Pine	73	YG-4-3-9
Spring Rose	39	RE-6-7-2
Spring White	68	GR-5-1-1
Sterling Blue	49	BV-9-6-7
Strawberry Parfait	32	RE-4-3-6
Summer Sky	58	BG-1-7-3
Sunflower	18	YE-5-5-2

Color Name	Pg#	TCS #
Sweetheart Pink	32	RE-4-3-4
Taffy	90	WH-8-2-6
Tangerine	20	YO-6-1-5
Tapioca	88	WH-6-3-2
Tartan Green	65	BG-9-6-8
Teal	61	BG-4-1-7
Teal Green	63	BG-5-7-6
Teddy Bear Brown	82	BR-6-4-7
Teddy Bear Tan	77	BR-1-2-3
Terra Cotta	23	OR-5-9-7
Thicket	73	YG-4-3-8
Thunder Blue	57	BL-7-4-9
True Blue	52	BL-5-1-5
True Burgundy (AP)	37	RE-6-4-9
Turner's Yellow (AP)	17	YE-5-4-5
Turquoise	62	BG-5-1-6
Victorian Rose	27	RO-5-3-1
Violet Pansy	45	VI-4-1-7
Warm White (AP)	90	WH-8-2-2
Whipped Berry	48	BV-6-8-3
White (Titanium) (AP)	88	WH-5-1-1
Wicker White	88	WH-5-1-2
Winter White	52	BL-5-1-1
Wintergreen	65	BG-9-6-9
Wrought Iron	69	GR-5-3-9
Yellow Light (AP)	17	YE-5-1-6
Yellow Ochre (AP)	19	YE-6-4-5

Jo Sonja® by Chroma

Color Name	Pg#	TCS #
Amethyst	44	RV-9-2-3
Antique Green	61	BG-4-7-8
Aqua	60	BG-4-1-5
Azure / Bkg.	48	BV-5-4-6
Black (Carbon)	86	BK-5-1-9
Blossom / Bkg.	26	RO-4-3-2
Brilliant Green	70	GR-7-2-5
Brilliant Magenta	41	RV-2-4-7
Brilliant Violet	46	VI-5-3-7
Brown Earth	80	BR-5-1-5
Brown Madder	32	RE-4-3-7
Burgundy	37	RE-6-4-9
Burnt Sienna	81	BR-6-2-6
Burnt Umber	84	BR-7-6-9
Cadmium Orange	26	RO-5-1-4
Cadmium Scarlet	31	RE-4-1-5
Cadmium Yellow Light	16	YE-4-1-4
Cadmium Yellow Mid	17	YE-5-1-6
Cashmere / Bkg.	23	OR-5-7-3
Celadon	62	BG-5-3-6
Charcoal / Bkg.	84	BR-8-6-8
Cobalt Blue Hue	56	BL-6-1-8
Colony Blue	59	BG-2-4-7

Color Name	Pg#	TCS #
Damask Rose / Bkg.	39	RE-6-7-7
Deep Plum / Bkg.	35	RE-5-6-9
Dioxazine Purple	46	VI-5-1-9
Dolphin Blue / Bkg.	51	BL-4-9-8
Dove Grey / Bkg.	85	BK-4-5-5
Fawn	81	BR-5-4-4
Forest Green / Bkg.	69	GR-5-3-9
French Blue	55	BL-5-7-8
Galaxy Blue / Bkg.	52	BL-4-9-9
Gold Oxide	22	OR-4-7-8
Green Light	71	GR-8-2-4
Green Oxide	72	GR-8-6-5
Holiday Green / Bkg.	66	GR-3-3-5
Holiday Red / Bkg.	31	RE-4-1-5
Hooker's Green	67	GR-3-5-8
Indian Red Oxide	35	RE-5-6-9
Indian Yellow	20	YO-5-1-4
Jade	68	GR-4-6-5
Jaune Brillant	21	OR-3-1-4
Lavender / Bkg.	44	RV-6-9-7
Light Teal / Bkg.	59	BG-2-4-9
Moss Green	76	YG-9-6-2
Naples Yellow Hue	19	YE-7-7-3
Napthol Crimson	36	RE-6-2-7
Napthol Red Light	31	RE-4-1-6
Nimbus Grey	85	BK-4-5-5
Norwegian Orange	28	RO-7-4-7
Oakmoss / Bkg.	86	BK-5-6-4
Olive Green	77	YG-9-9-9
Olive Green / Bkg.	76	YG-9-8-7
Opal	83	BR-7-6-3
Pacific Blue	49	BV-8-3-6
Payne's Grey	53	BL-5-2-9
Permanent Alizarin	37	RE-6-4-8
Pine Green	73	YG-4-3-8
Plum Pink	38	RE-6-5-7
Primrose / Bkg.	19	YE-7-7-3
Provincial Beige	80	BR-4-4-4
Prussian Blue Hue	53	BL-5-2-7
Pthalo Blue	53	BL-5-2-6
Pthalo Green	65	BG-9-1-8
Purple Madder	40	RE-7-2-9
Raw Sienna	77	BR-1-2-4
Raw Umber	84	BR-8-6-8
Red Earth	33	RE-4-6-5
Red Violet	40	RV-1-2-6
Rose Pink	32	RE-4-3-8
Rosehip / Bkg.	23	OR-5-9-8
Sap Green	70	GR-7-4-5
Sapphire	50	BL-4-5-6
Skintone Base	23	OR-5-9-3
Sky Blue / Bkg.	54	BL-5-7-3
Smoked Pearl	89	WH-6-4-6
Soft White / Bkg.	90	WH-8-2-2
Spice / Bkg.	33	RE-4-6-5
Storm Blue	52	BL-4-9-9
Teal Green	66	BG-9-7-9

	Pg#	TCS#
Trans. Magenta	40	RV-1-2-7
Turner's Yellow	18	YE-6-2-6
Ultramarine Blue	52	BL-5-1-5
Ultramarine Blue Deep	52	BL-5-1-6
Unbleached Titanium	22	OR-5-2-1
Vellum / Bkg.	88	WH-3-7-7
Vermillion	26	RO-5-1-7
Victorian Green / Bkg.	65	BG-9-6-9
Victorian Red / Bkg.	36	RE-6-2-8
Warm White	90	WH-8-2-2
White (Titanium)	88	WH-5-1-1
Yellow Deep	20	YO-5-2-4
Yellow Light	17	YE-5-1-5
Yellow Oxide	19	YE-6-4-7

1837 Legacy® by Maple Ridge

Color Name	Pg#	TCS #
1837 Green	73	YG-4-3-3
Aegean Blue	54	BL-5-5-5
Algonquin Green	72	GR-8-6-6
Amethyst	44	RV-9-2-3
Antique Green	72	YG-4-3-2
Antique Lace	89	WH-6-4-2
Apache	79	BR-2-4-6
Apricot	25	RO-1-3-3
Aqua	60	BG-4-1-2
Arrowhead	85	BK-3-7-5
Artichoke	74	YG-5-6-6
Atlantic Surf	58	BG-1-7-2
Autumn Leaf	30	RE-3-2-7
Banana Cream	16	YE-4-1-3
Banff Blue	54	BL-5-7-3
Barley	16	YE-2-4-2
Bay Leaf	73	YG-4-3-9
Big Sky	57	BG-1-3-2
Bing Cherry	31	RE-4-2-5
Birch White	90	WH-8-2-2
Black	85	BK-5-1-8
Black Angus	86	BK-5-1-9
Black Green	69	GR-5-3-9
Black Ruby	35	RE-5-6-9
Blarney	68	GR-4-6-5
Blazer Blue	53	BL-5-2-6
Blue Birds	53	BL-5-2-4
Brick	28	RO-5-4-7
Brown Iron Oxide	80	BR-5-1-5
Brown Sugar	78	BR-1-3-5
Burgundy	37	RE-6-4-9
Burnt Almond	83	BR-7-6-3
Burnt Clay	28	RO-5-4-4
Burnt Sienna	81	BR-6-2-5
Burnt Umber	83	BR-7-5-8
Cameo Pink	31	RE-4-3-1
Canola	16	YE-4-1-2
Cappuccino	78	BR-2-2-4
Caribou	18	YE-5-5-5
Carnation Pink	35	RE-6-2-3
Cashmere Rose	29	RO-8-3-4
Chamois	19	YE-7-7-4
Cherub	25	RO-2-3-3
Chestnut	80	BR-5-1-6
Chrome Green Light	72	GR-8-6-5
Cinnabar	34	RE-5-5-8
Clover Green	71	GR-8-2-3
Cool Blue	60	BG-3-4-3
Cool Peach	21	OR-4-7-3
Corn Silk	24	OR-6-3-2
Coronado Red	31	RE-4-1-6
Country Slate Blue	55	BL-5-8-7
Cove Blue	62	BG-5-3-7
Cranberry	37	RE-6-4-8
Creamette	90	WH-8-2-3
Creamy Beige	78	BR-2-2-2
Cypress Green	64	BG-8-6-2
Daffodil	17	YE-5-2-3
Damsel Rose	27	RO-5-3-2
Dandelion	17	YE-5-1-7
Dark Brown Sugar	79	BR-2-2-8
Dark Evergreen	62	BG-5-1-8
Dark Sapphire Blue	55	BL-5-7-9
Daybreak	36	RE-6-2-4
Delft Blue	54	BL-5-7-4
Desert Tea	23	OR-5-5-3
Devon Cream	90	WH-8-2-6
Doeskin	81	BR-5-4-4
Dove Grey	87	BK-7-2-3
Dover Blue	54	BL-5-7-5
Duck Bill	22	OR-5-1-5
Dusty Rose	25	OR-6-7-4
Ecru	22	OR-5-2-1
Electric Blue	49	BV-9-1-8
Emerald Green	70	GR-7-2-5
Emeraude	64	BG-8-6-4
Empire Green	75	YG-8-8-7
Erin Green	69	GR-6-2-5
Espresso	84	BR-8-6-8
Eucalyptus	62	BG-5-3-8
Evergreen	72	GR-8-6-8
Faded Rose	33	RE-4-4-3
Festive Pink	30	RE-3-2-5
Fire Truck Red	35	RE-6-1-5
Flesh	81	BR-5-4-2
Foliage Green	61	BG-4-7-8
Forest Night	65	BG-9-6-9
Forget-Me-Not Blue	48	BV-8-3-4
French Blue Grey	51	BL-4-8-5
Fresh Tangerine	26	RO-5-1-6
Fundy Blue	58	BG-1-7-5
Garland	72	YG-3-2-6
Gentle Blue	56	BL-6-1-3
Geranium Red	39	RE-7-2-5
Glacial Lake	60	BG-4-1-4
Golden Gourd	79	BR-2-4-4
Golden Rod	18	YE-6-2-6
Grecian Rose	39	RE-6-7-7
Green Olive	74	YG-5-6-7
Green Tea	74	YG-6-2-3
Grit Red	28	RO-7-4-7
Hansa Yellow	17	YE-5-1-5
Hazelnut	82	BR-6-4-5
Heavenly Blue	52	BL-5-2-2
Hedge Row	67	GR-3-3-6
Holly Green	69	GR-5-4-7
Holly Hock	63	BG-7-1-2
Hunter Green	62	BG-4-7-9
Iris	45	VI-5-1-4
Irish Green	70	GR-6-4-5
Ivory Cream	23	OR-5-7-3
Ivy	73	YG-4-3-8
Jasper	68	GR-3-7-4
Kohl Blue	52	BL-4-9-9
Lavender	45	VI-5-1-5
Lemon Meringue	18	YE-6-2-2
Light Rose	23	OR-5-9-7
Light Yellow Green	75	YG-9-2-3
Lilac Grey	43	RV-5-8-2
Lime	71	GR-8-2-4
Lupin Pink	39	RE-6-7-4
Madder Rose	30	RE-3-5-5
Maiden's Blush	27	RO-5-3-3
Maize	16	YE-4-1-1
Manganese Blue	56	BL-7-2-8
Mango	21	OR-4-1-5
Margarine	19	YE-7-7-3
Marshland	66	GR-1-4-1
Medium Flesh	24	OR-6-3-5
Milk Chocolate	82	BR-6-4-4
Mocha	78	BR-2-2-5
Moss	73	YG-4-3-6
Mountain Blue	60	BG-4-1-5
Mountie Red	35	RE-6-1-6
Mulberry	43	RV-5-8-8
Myrtle Green	67	GR-3-7-3
Napthol Crimson	34	RE-5-1-6
Napthol Red Light	36	RE-6-2-6
Natural Blush	24	OR-6-3-3
Nordic Blue	59	BG-1-7-8
Nutmeg	79	BR-2-2-6
Oak	80	BR-2-5-4
Oatmeal	90	WH-8-2-8
Olive Branch	75	YG-8-8-4
Olivette	76	YG-9-8-7
Ontario Blue	50	BL-4-5-6
Opal	25	OR-6-7-3
Orange	26	RO-5-1-7
Oxford Grey	51	BL-4-8-4
Pacifica	59	BG-2-4-7
Pansey Purple	43	RV-5-8-5
Paprika	28	RO-5-4-5

Peachee	22	OR-5-3-4	Thalo Blue	52	BL-5-1-5
Pelican	87	BK-6-2-2	Tigereye	19	YE-6-4-8
Peony Pink	30	RE-3-5-3	Toast	82	BR-6-4-2
Persian Red	31	RE-4-1-5	Tory Blue	56	BL-6-1-5
Pewter	85	BK-3-7-8	Tundra	80	BR-4-4-4
Phantom Blue	55	BL-5-7-8	Valentine	37	RE-6-4-4
Pink Begonia	42	RV-3-2-4	Velvet Night	53	BL-5-2-8
Pioneer Grey	51	BL-4-9-5	Velvet Plum	42	RV-3-2-7
Plum	44	RV-9-2-9	Warm Beige	78	BR-2-2-3
Plum Wine	43	RV-5-9-8	Warm Brown	79	BR-2-2-7
Potpourri Rose	39	RE-6-7-5	Wedgewood Blue	54	BL-5-5-3
Potter's Clay	77	BR-1-2-3	Wedgewood Green	69	GR-5-6-4
Pottery	25	OR-6-3-8	Wheat	20	YO-6-1-1
Prairie Green	69	GR-5-4-6	White	88	WH-5-1-1
Prussian Blue	56	BL-7-2-9	Wild Berry	32	RE-4-3-7
Pthalo Crimson	36	RE-6-2-8	Wild Rose	29	RE-3-2-2
Pthalo Green	65	BG-9-1-8	Winter Wine	38	RE-6-5-7
Pumpkin Pie	21	OR-4-7-6	Yellow Oxide	19	YE-6-4-7
Purple	45	VI-5-1-7			
Purple Sage	43	RV-5-8-4			
Raspberry	37	RE-6-4-7			
Raw Sienna	77	BR-1-2-5			
Raw Umber	84	BR-8-5-7			
Red Iron Oxide	33	RE-4-6-5			
Red Pepper	23	OR-5-9-8			
Rhino Grey	86	BK-5-5-5			
Ripe Tomato	31	RE-4-2-6			
Rose Dawn	30	RE-3-5-7			
Rouge	29	RE-3-2-4			
Russet	27	RO-5-2-5			
Sage	71	GR-7-9-4			
Salmon	23	OR-5-9-6			
Sandy Peach	25	OR-6-7-2			
Sapphire Blue	56	BL-6-1-6			
Sea Shell Pink	32	RE-4-3-3			
Shrub	73	YG-4-3-7			
Shy Violet	48	BV-7-8-3			
Silver Fox	85	BK-4-5-5			
Skin Tone	24	OR-6-3-4			
Slate Grey	50	BL-3-8-8			
Smoky Blue	51	BL-4-9-8			
Snowball	55	BL-6-1-2			
Soft Kohl	87	BK-6-2-9			
Soft Lilac	44	RV-9-6-1			
Spiced Peach	24	OR-6-3-6			
Spider Web	89	WH-6-4-6			
Spring Green	75	YG-8-2-2			
St. Clair Blue	61	BG-4-4-5			
Sterling Grey	85	BK-3-7-4			
Storm Cloud	86	BK-5-5-3			
Sumac Red	31	RE-4-2-7			
Sunflower	16	YE-4-1-4			
Sungold	17	YE-5-4-5			
Superior Blue	51	BL-4-8-8			
Sweet Cream	90	WH-8-2-4			
Taupe	83	BR-7-4-3			
Terra Rosa	39	RE-6-8-4			

OILS

Archival® Oils by Chroma

Color Name	Pg#	TCS #
Archival Crimson	34	RE-5-1-6
Arylomide Yellow Deep	20	YO-5-1-4
Black (Mars)	86	BK-5-1-9
Brilliant Magenta	41	RV-2-4-7
Brilliant Orange	26	RO-5-1-4
Brown Earth	83	BR-7-6-8
Burnt Sienna	81	BR-6-2-6
Burnt Umber	84	BR-7-6-9
Cadmium Orange	22	OR-5-1-5
Cadmium Red Mid	36	RE-6-2-7
Cadmium Scarlet	31	RE-4-1-5
Cadmium Yellow Light	16	YE-4-1-4
Cadmium Yellow Mid	17	YE-5-1-6
Cerulean Blue Hue	56	BL-6-1-6
Chromium Green Oxide	72	GR-8-6-5
Cobalt Blue	56	BL-6-1-8
Cobalt Blue Hue	53	BL-5-2-5
Cobalt Turquoise	60	BG-4-1-5
Dioxazine Violet	46	VI-5-1-9
Forest Green	66	BG-9-7-9
Gold Ochre	22	OR-4-7-8
Indian Red	37	RE-6-4-8
Indian Yellow	21	OR-4-1-5
Jaune Brillant	20	YO-6-1-1
Light Red Oxide	28	RO-7-4-7
Mars Violet	38	RE-6-5-8
Naples Yellow Hue	78	BR-2-2-2
Napthol Crimson	36	RE-6-2-8
Napthol Scarlet	31	RE-4-1-6
Olive Green	77	YG-9-9-9
Payne's Grey	53	BL-5-2-9
Permanent Alizarin	37	RE-6-4-9
Permanent Brown Madder	31	RE-4-2-7
Permanent Green Light	71	GR-8-2-4
Permanent Magenta	41	RV-1-2-8
Permanent Sap Green	70	GR-7-4-5
Permanent Viridian Hue	65	BG-9-6-9
Prussian Blue	53	BL-5-2-7
Pthalo Blue	53	BL-5-2-6
Pthalo Green	65	BG-9-1-9
Pthalo Green (Yellow Shade)	65	BG-9-1-8
Pthalo Turquoise	59	BG-2-4-7
Purple Madder	40	RE-7-2-9
Quinacridone Red Violet	40	RV-1-2-7
Raw Sienna	77	BR-1-2-4
Raw Umber	84	BR-8-6-8
Red Gold	28	RO-5-4-4
Royal Blue	49	BV-9-6-9
Sky Blue	52	BL-5-1-5
Superchrome Scarlet	26	RO-5-1-7
Superchrome Yellow Light	17	YE-4-1-5
Superchrome Yellow Mid	17	YE-5-1-7
Transparent Red Oxide	35	RE-5-6-9
Ultramarine Blue	52	BL-5-1-6
Violet Grey	50	BL-3-8-8
Warm Grey	87	BK-6-2-8
White (Sft. Formula Titanium)	88	WH-5-1-2
White (Titanium)	88	WH-5-1-1
Yellow Green	76	YG-9-4-6
Yellow Light	17	YE-5-1-5
Yellow Ochre	19	YE-6-4-5
Zinc White	90	WH-8-2-2
Not included:		
Burnt Orange Quinacridone		RO-3-3-8

Prima® Oils by Martin/F.Weber

Color Name	Pg#	TCS #
Alizarin Crimson	37	RE-6-4-8
Black (Ivory)	85	BK-5-1-8
Burnt Sienna	81	BR-6-2-6
Burnt Umber	84	BR-7-6-9
Cadmium Red Light Hue	26	RO-5-1-7
Cadmium Red Medium Hue	34	RE-5-1-6
Cadmium Yellow Light Hue	17	YE-5-1-7
Cadmium Yellow Med. Hue	20	YO-6-1-5
Cerulean Blue Hue	57	BG-1-3-8
Cobalt Blue Hue	53	BL-5-2-5
Cobalt Violet Hue	44	RV-9-2-9
Emerald Green	73	YG-4-3-6
Naples Yellow Hue	19	YE-7-7-4
Peach (Light Flesh)	24	OR-6-3-3
Phthalo Green	65	BG-9-6-9
Prima Gray	86	BK-5-5-3
Prima Pink	30	RE-3-2-6
Raw Sienna	78	BR-1-2-7
Sap Green	70	GR-7-4-5
Turquoise	61	BG-4-4-5
Ultramarine Blue	53	BL-5-2-6

Color Name	Pg#	TCS #
Van Dyke Brown	84	BR-8-6-9
White (Titanium)	88	WH-5-1-2
Yellow Ochre	80	BR-2-5-8

Rembrandt® Oils by Talens

Color Name	Pg#	TCS #
ACRA Red	37	RE-6-4-4
Alizarin Crimson	37	RE-6-4-9
Barrick Flesh Blush	29	RO-8-3-4
Barrick Flesh Medium	25	OR-6-7-3
Black (Ivory)	85	BK-5-1-8
Blue Green	61	BG-4-1-8
Brownish Madder (Alizarin)	32	RE-4-3-7
Burnt Carmine	40	RE-7-2-9
Burnt Umber	83	BR-7-5-8
Cad. Yellow Med.	17	YE-5-1-7
Cadmium Red Light	27	RO-5-1-8
Cadmium Yellow Light	16	YE-4-1-4
Cinnabar Green	75	YG-8-2-2
Cobalt Blue Light	56	BL-6-1-8
Emerald Green	70	GR-6-4-5
Flesh Ochre	28	RO-5-4-7
Geranium Lake	26	RO-5-1-7
Greenish Umber	69	GR-5-3-8
Indigo	52	BL-4-9-9
Indigo Extra	56	BL-7-2-9
Madder Lake	37	RE-6-4-8
Naples Yellow Light	18	YE-6-2-2
Olive Green	73	YG-4-3-7
Payne's Gray	53	BL-5-2-9
Permanent Brown Madder	35	RE-5-6-9
Raw Sienna	77	BR-1-2-4
Raw Umber	84	BR-8-6-8
Rembrandt Rose	36	RE-6-2-7
Rembrandt Yellow	74	YG-7-3-2
Rose Madder Antique	33	RE-4-4-3
Sap Green	71	GR-8-3-9
Stil De Grain Brun	79	BR-2-2-8
Stil De Grain Jaune	20	YO-5-1-4
Trans. Oxide Brown	84	BR-7-6-9
Transparent Oxide Red	83	BR-7-6-8
Turquoise Blue	60	BG-4-1-5
Viridian	65	BG-9-1-8
Warm Grey	84	BK-1-7-8
White (Titanium)	88	WH-5-1-1
Yellow Ochre	80	BR-2-5-8
Yellow Ochre Lt.	19	YE-6-4-5

This partial list of Rembrandt Oil Colors reflects only those included in this sourcebook.

Winsor & Newton® Oils

Color Name	Pg#	TCS #
Aureolin	18	YE-6-2-6
Black (Lamp)	86	BK-5-1-9
Black (Ivory)	85	BK-5-1-8
Bright Red	34	RE-5-1-4
Brown Madder Alizarin	80	BR-5-1-5
Burnt Sienna	81	BR-6-2-5
Burnt Umber	83	BR-7-5-8
Cadmium Green	70	GR-7-2-5
Cadmium Green Pale	75	YG-8-2-2
Cadmium Lemon	16	YE-4-1-4
Cadmium Orange	22	OR-5-1-5
Cadmium Red	36	RE-6-2-6
Cadmium Red Deep	36	RE-6-2-8
Cadmium Yellow	20	YO-5-2-4
Cadmium Yellow Deep	20	YO-6-1-5
Cadmium Yellow Pale	17	YE-4-1-5
Carmine	36	RE-6-2-7
Cerulean Blue	57	BG-1-3-8
Charcoal Grey	87	BK-6-2-9
Chrome Green Deep Hue	69	GR-5-4-7
Chrome Yellow Hue	17	YE-5-1-6
Cobalt Blue	56	BL-6-1-8
Cobalt Green	63	BG-7-1-3
Cobalt Green Deep	65	BG-9-6-8
Cobalt Turquoise	61	BG-4-2-8
Cobalt Violet	42	RV-5-2-7
Cobalt Violet Dark	44	RV-9-2-8
Davy's Gray	76	YG-9-9-3
Flesh Tint	27	RO-5-3-3
French Ultramarine	52	BL-5-1-6
Gold Ochre	80	BR-2-5-8
Indanthrene Blue	52	BL-5-1-9
Indian Red	33	RE-4-6-5
Indian Yellow	20	YO-5-1-4
Indigo	53	BL-5-2-9
Jaune Brillant	21	OR-3-1-4
Lemon Yellow Hue	16	YE-2-4-2
Magenta	42	RV-2-4-8
Mars Orange	28	RO-5-4-5
Mars Violet	33	RE-4-6-7
Mars Violet Deep	34	RE-5-5-8
Mars Yellow	19	YE-6-4-5
Mauve (Blue Shade)	46	VI-5-1-9
Naples Yellow Light	18	YE-6-2-2
Olive Green	76	YG-9-8-7
Oxide of Chromium	67	GR-3-5-7
Payne's Gray	52	BL-4-9-9
Perm. Alizarin Crimson	41	RV-1-2-8
Permanent Green	66	GR-3-2-4
Permanent Green Light	69	GR-6-2-5
Permanent Magenta	41	RV-2-4-7
Permanent Mauve	43	RV-5-8-9
Permanent Rose	40	RV-1-2-5
Phthalo Turquoise	61	BG-4-1-8

Color Name	Pg#	TCS #
Prussian Blue	56	BL-7-2-8
Prussian Green	67	GR-3-6-8
Purple Lake	40	RE-7-2-9
Purple Madder Alizarin	42	RV-3-2-8
Raw Sienna	77	BR-1-2-5
Raw Umber	84	BR-8-5-7
Rose Dore	27	RO-5-3-4
Rose Madder Deep	32	RE-4-3-8
Rose Madder Genuine	32	RE-4-3-6
Sap Green	72	YG-3-2-6
Scarlet Lake	26	RO-5-1-7
Terra Rosa	28	RO-5-4-7
Terre Verte	69	GR-5-4-6
Transparent Yellow	17	YE-5-2-3
Ultramarine Green Shade	56	BL-6-1-6
Ultramarine Violet	46	VI-5-3-7
Vandyke Brown	84	BR-7-6-9
Venetian Red	22	OR-4-7-9
Vermilion Hue	31	RE-4-1-6
Viridian	62	BG-5-1-6
White (Titanium)	88	WH-5-1-1
Winsor Blue Red Shade	52	BL-5-1-5
Winsor Emerald	63	BG-7-1-6
Winsor Green	65	BG-9-1-8
Winsor Green (Yellow Shade)	66	GR-3-3-5
Winsor Lemon	17	YE-5-1-5
Winsor Orange	26	RO-5-1-4
Winsor Red	27	RO-5-1-8
Winsor Red Deep	34	RE-5-1-6
Winsor Violet (Dioxazine)	45	VI-5-1-7
Winsor Yellow	18	YE-6-2-4
Yellow Ochre	19	YE-6-4-8
Yellow Ochre Pale	19	YE-6-4-7

The following Winsor & Newton Oil Colors not included in this sourcebook are listed below with their assigned TCS#'s.

Color Name	TCS #
Alizarin Crimson	RE-6-2-9
Black (Mars)	BK-4-1-9
Blue Black	BL-5-4-9
Cadmium Scarlet	RO-7-1-6
Cobalt Blue Deep	BV-9-1-6
Manganese Blue Hue	BG-4-3-5
Mars Brown	BR-2-2-9
Naples Yellow	YE-6-4-4
Permanent Green Deep	BG-8-2-8
Permanent Sap Green	YG-3-2-5
Transparent Gold Ochre	YO-2-1-3
Winsor Blue Green Shade	BL-8-2-8
Winsor Yellow Deep	YO-5-2-5

HERE ARE ALL THE TCS© IDENTIFIERS

COLOR	HUE	CLARITY 1-bright	VALUE 1-light
YE = Yellow	1	1	1
YO = Yellow-Orange			
OR = Orange	2	2	2
RO = Red-Orange			
RE = Red	3	3	3
RV = Red-Violet	4	4	4
VI = Violet			
BV = Blue-Violet	5	5	5
BL = Blue			
BG = Blue-Green	6	6	6
GR = Green	7	7	7
YG = Yellow-Green			
BR = Brown	8	8	8
BK = Black			
WH = White	9	9	9
FAMILIES	5=pure color	to 9-muted	to 9-dark

Illustrated Examples

RE-3-2-5
Genesis Oils	Pyrrole Red 05
1837 Legacy	Festive Pink
Accent	Cottage Rose

BG-4-4-5
Americana	Desert Turquoise
Prima Oils	Turquoise
Max Oil	Cobalt Turquoise

GR-8-6-6
Ceramcoat	Forest Green
Folk Art	Old Ivy
Duo Aqua Oil	Sap Green

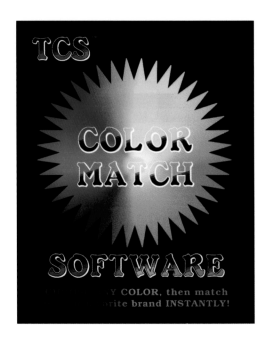

TCS COLOR MATCH SOFTWARE

5,500 Oil / Acrylic colors & mixes with ratios

- Computer solution to color conversions.
- Find any color, then match to your favorite brand instantly!
- No charts to shuffle, no pages to search.
- Suggested shade and highlight in many brands.
- Includes manufacturer's number so you can easily find the target color on the retailer's rack.

Eliminate the guesswork and doubts since your computer can tell you the color equivalents in the brands you choose to survey. It will print the results and inventory of the colors you own.

See page 13 for the brands featured in this software.

$49.95 each + $5.00 S/H
For all Windows Systems

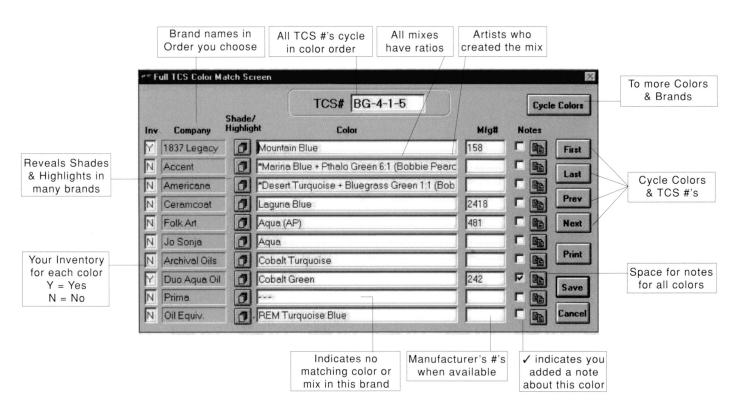

This screen image shows nine (9) names & mixes – all the same color

TCS PAINTER'S LIBRARY

- **Helps you get organized . . .**it's easy. This software is designed to help you get your painting books, pattern packets and magazine projects in order – and give you their location.

- **Sorts** your entire library into subject matter so you can choose from flowers, landscapes, santas or any category you desire.

- **Includes inventory listing** of your on-hand painting supplies and creates a personal shopping list of the items you need to buy.

Set up your own filing system, then enter key information about the project or book. Now you can find it by author, title, publication, even location and category. Plus, you can establish your own classifications.

Now, when you see a beautiful wood, tin or fabric item you wish to paint, look in your Painter's Library to find just the right pattern. It's easy to select the best – only the ones you want to paint.

$49.95 each + $5.00 S/H
For all Windows Systems

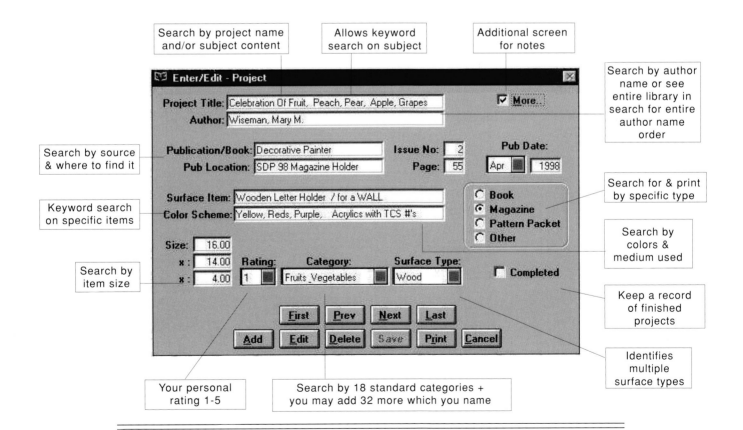

Search by project name and/or subject content

Allows keyword search on subject

Additional screen for notes

Search by author name or see entire library in search for entire author name order

Search by source & where to find it

Keyword search on specific items

Search by item size

Search for & print by specific type

Search by colors & medium used

Keep a record of finished projects

Identifies multiple surface types

Your personal rating 1-5

Search by 18 standard categories + you may add 32 more which you name

DECORATIVE PAINTERS GROW BY TEACHING OTHERS!

Many painters are excited about the possibilities of sharing the fun and enjoyment of painting. The *Tru-Color Teaching Guide & Session Planner©* is a "How To" manual which outlines a practical plan from organizing your classes to choosing and designing your class projects.

The
Art
of
Decorative
Painting

Teaching Guide and Session Planner©

This comprehensive three-ring binder is packed with ideas, step-by-step instructions, sample documents, and valuable information to help you develop a sound program for teaching decorative painting.

Lays out a practical approach to successful classes, including:
- 10 Qualities of Effective Teaching - simple ground rules
- How to Inspire Your Students to Learn
- Where to Teach - pros & cons of each option
- Planning Your Sessions - sample agendas
- Coaching and Illustrating Basic Strokes
- The Importance of the Color Wheel
- Setting, Communicating and Reaching Session Objectives
- What Prospective Students Want to Know Before Committing
- The Tru-Color Session Planner - a proven blueprint
- The Importance of "Attitude" - YOURS!

Involvement in teaching means you will be in the company of people who understand your interests. You will share (and learn) new ideas as you develop additional skills to pass along to your students. Order your personal copy today and receive a

FREE STUDENT GUIDE

$19.95 (U.S. funds)
plus S/H: U.S. $5.00 - Canada $8.00
International: Ask for Quote

Ten (10) Reasons to Order ... TODAY!

1. You'll see immediate benefits from the practical principles and strategies which are presented.

2. Covers all the bases for developing a unified game plan for your "first" or "best" class ever.

3. Learn to recognize and avoid common planning mistakes which cause teachers to stumble.

4. No need to travel to an expensive seminar location we deliver the information to your door.

5. You will learn tips, techniques and hands-on methods which you can put to work right away.

6. Build highly effective session plans which will give you enthusiasm to complete classes successfully.

7. Demystify teachers methods, "by planning like a pro" – it's simpler than you think.

8. Learn how every teacher can "build-in" flexibility to deal with the inevitable change in plans.

9. This three-ring binder will be a living document as you add information for many years into the future.

10. You will get a substantial return from a very small investment.

Tru-Color Systems, Inc.

P.O. Box 486 • Danville, IN 46122-0486
Phone: 317.745.7535 Fax: 317.745.1886 E-mail: order@gotcs.com

GUARANTEE
Our guarantee is simple. If you are not completely satisfied that these books "deliver" as promised, simply return within five (5) days for a complete refund of $19.95.

"If you are a beginning teacher, buy this book. Even if you are an experienced teacher, buy this book. Very thorough publication - Well worth the asking price."

Business Report
Society of Decorative Painters.

Tru-Color Comparison Discs

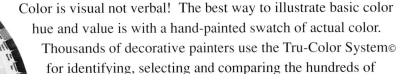

See for yourself . . .

Color is visual not verbal! The best way to illustrate basic color hue and value is with a hand-painted swatch of actual color. Thousands of decorative painters use the Tru-Color System© for identifying, selecting and comparing the hundreds of different choices which are available.

The Tru-Color Comparison Disc© is a collection of hand-painted swatches featuring the most popular colors used by the artist. The swatches are painted on circular discs for comparison with corresponding or similar colors. A simple rotation of the discs allows you to compare hundreds of actual paint swatches grouped by color and brand. Contact us for more information.

. . . Seeing is believing!

Door/Wall-Hung Paint Rack

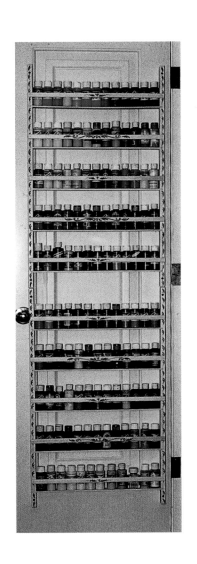

Out of the way, yet handy, too!
Paint storage – now there is a better way.

- Easily installs on the inside of any door or mounts on the wall.
- Holds 130 bottles of paint.
- Includes two 35" modules – ten shelves (19 1/2" wide)
- Contains complete step-by-step assembly instructions.
- Needs only a hammer and screwdriver.
- This wood paint rack can be decorated and installed all by yourself.

Quick and Efficient Paint Storage

This unique paint rack is easily mounted on any standard-height door or on a wall. It is built to hold two-ounce paint bottles. It can also be modified to accommodate jars and tubes. (Basswood / 24 pcs.)

Paints can be stored by color and brand for easy access.
Make it easy by arranging your paint in TCS#.

Full-Door module .... $37.95 + S/H

(Shipping/Handling: $7.00 U.S., $12.00 Canada U.S. Funds)

Visit our World Wide Web page on the Internet:
Calendar of Events for Decorative Painters
Studios & Shops listed by state, province or country
www.gotcs.com

Notes